# XD
# OPERATIONS

# XD OPERATIONS

## Secret British Missions Denying Oil to the Nazis

by

## CLIFFORD BRAZIER

Edited by

## P. H. Brazier

Pen & Sword
**MILITARY**

First published in Great Britain in 2004 by
Pen & Sword Military
an imprint of
Pen & Sword Books Ltd
47 Church Street
Barnsley
South Yorkshire
S70 2AS

ISBN 1 84415 136 0

A CIP catalogue record for this book is
available from the British Library

Typeset in Sabon by Phoenix Typesetting, Auldgirth, Dumfriesshire
Printed and bound in England by
CPI UK

Pen & Sword Books Ltd incorporates the imprints of Pen & Sword Aviation,
Pen & Sword Maritime, Pen & Sword Military, Wharncliffe Local History,
Pen and Sword Select, Pen and Sword Military Classics and Leo Cooper.

For a complete list of Pen & Sword titles please contact
PEN & SWORD BOOKS LIMITED
47 Church Street, Barnsley, South Yorkshire, S70 2AS, England
E-mail: enquiries@pen-and-sword.co.uk
Website: www.pen-and-sword.co.uk

Dedicated to the officers and men of
The Kent Fortress Royal Engineers TA,
who answered the call on 3 September 1939.


'*War is an ugly thing, but not the ugliest of things:*
*the decayed and degraded state of moral and patriotic*
*feeling which thinks nothing worth a war, is worse.*'

J.S. MILL

# CONTENTS

# FOREWORD

by Professor Richard Holmes, CBE, TD

I am particularly pleased to have been asked to write the foreword to this book. As a military historian I am delighted to see an almost unknown aspect of the Second World War given the attention it deserves, and as a former Territorial I am proud to acknowledge the remarkable achievements of a Territorial Army unit.

The title 'Kent Fortress Royal Engineers' has a wonderfully old-fashioned ring, but in fact the unit bearing it dated only from 1932 when the government decided to make Territorials, rather than regulars, responsible for the defence of Britain's coasts against enemy attack. Its ranks were filled with volunteers in just forty-eight hours, thanks largely to the efforts of its commanding officer, Clifford Brazier, the author of this book.

In 1940 the Kent Fortress Royal Engineers were tasked, at short notice and in extreme secrecy, with wrecking oil storage facilities in France and the Low Countries. The task demanded the destruction of the large fuel oil stocks along the coastline from Holland to the Bay of Biscay. These would have represented a great prize for the German war machine. Sites which were often close to areas which had to remain undamaged, sometimes with understandable local tension about the demolitions, and often with a high risk of air attack and the close proximity of advancing German troops. It required not only specialist knowledge, but also a high degree of courage and resourcefulness. Officers and NCOs often had to act on their own initiative: the buck stopped with them. Although the demands of national security meant that the unit's considerable achievement could not be reported at the time, the achievement of the Kent Fortress Royal Engineers was recognized with a list of awards which made it, for the time, the most decorated unit in the British army.

The unit's contribution to victory did not end there. It was in Kent during the Blitz; sent a detachment on a Commando raid to Spitzbergen; provided the nucleus for a parachute engineer squadron and elements served in the North African desert. However the bulk of the original unit returned to France by way of Normandy to fight through Belgium and Holland and on into Germany. All this would have been a remarkable achievement for regular soldiers, but so many of these men had begun as part-time soldiers, and at the end of the war the survivors returned to the communities they had defended so well. Before the war it had been easy to poke fun at Territorials as 'Saturday night soldiers,' but after it Field Marshal Slim aptly affirmed that the Territorial was actually 'twice a citizen'.

As I write these lines members of the Territorial Army are serving abroad on operations on a scale not seen since the Second World War. Sometimes they are specialists, adding value to Britain's contribution by making use of their own civilian expertise, and sometimes, by doing purely military tasks, they are taking some of the strain off a busy regular army. This book reminds us that the army has a long history of blending Territorials and regulars in a rich mixture that represents the best of two distinct but complementary military traditions.

# INTRODUCTION

In the spring of 1940, the country learnt with relief of the miracle of Dunkirk and the courage of the Royal Navy and flotillas of small ships that plucked our army from the beaches. Churchill and his military advisers knew, however, that there was little to celebrate. In just a few weeks Hitler, with his blitzkrieg, had achieved what the Kaiser had failed to do in four years – he had overrun France and crushed her armed forces and swept ours from mainland Europe. Britain stood alone against the might of Nazi Germany.

General Sir Richard Gale, who commanded 1 Parachute Brigade and later 6th Airborne Division on D Day, was a Colonel on the staff of the Director of Military Operations at the War Office in 1940. In his autobiography *Call to Arms* he wrote of this dark period:

> *The withdrawal from France and the evacuation from Dunkirk was no direct concern of ours . . . . The tragedy of these events were for us, however, off-set to some extent by the exploits of a Territorial Army Unit, the Kent Fortress Engineers, with whose work we were intimately concerned. Their exploits are little known, which for reasons of security at the time is not surprising.*
>
> *These operations were no less than the destruction of all oil installations in the Low Countries and northern France. The task had to be done by small parties of men who remained behind after the army had withdrawn, subsequently making their getaway as best they could. Some we managed to get off by destroyer; others only made their escape weeks later after the Germans were in the whole of northern France.*

General Gale continued:

*The firing of oil installations is not simple if this is to be done in such a way that the conflagration caused cannot be put down. It takes time, requires detailed knowledge of the installation, great skill and above all courage. These qualities the officers and men of this unit had in good measure.*

Who was this unit and why were they given the largest demolition programme ever undertaken by the Royal Engineers? How did they become the most highly decorated unit (150 all ranks) at that time in the British Army?

In 1932 to save regular manpower in the army, the War Office decided to replace the regular gunner and sapper units manning our coastal defences, with local recruited Territorial units. The War Office approached the Managing Director, A.C. Davis, of the Blue Circle Cement Company to sponsor a company sized Territorial unit for this purpose. At that time the author of this book, my father Clifford Brazier, was manager of their largest cement works in Kent. As he had served as a sapper officer in the First World War and had left the army afterwards as a major, he was asked to raise and command the unit which was named The Kent Fortress Royal Engineers. In the event it was raised to full strength in forty-eight hours; a record which has never been equalled! Initially the unit was almost exclusively drawn from personnel working in the local Blue Circle cement works. They became highly regarded by the military authorities for their efficiency and in 1938 my father was made a brevet lieutenant colonel. He remained in command until handing over on promotion in February 1942. This is simply the story of this TA sapper unit through the first two and a half years of the war.

These operations, code named XD, were highly secret at the time mainly because of their political sensitivity. As a result when my father, just after handing over command, wrote this book based on reports and conversations with his officers and men and his own experiences of the operations, he was not able to mention the names of the players or much of the details of the tasks. Although this book is, in general, much as he wrote it, I have altered it in places for authenticity as far as possible and have been able to put in the correct names where they are known. I have deliberately not removed references to Huns, Jerries and Boche as these were the terms used at that time. The sentiments expressed reflected the prevailing national mood. It is worth remembering that my father's generation had to take up arms against the Germans twice in their lifetime.

Sadly, few of the people mentioned are still alive, I am however greatly indebted for the help and encouragement given to me in particular by Major Peter Keeble DSO MC TD, who was one of the main players in this saga. At the age of ninety-three his memory of those days is quite remarkable considering it was sixty-three years ago. I am also indebted to Lieutenant Colonel Paul Baker MBE, who was one of the first young officers to join the Kent Fortress unit straight from officer training only days before their first operation. The other person who has been of help is Barry Phillips, until recently the Chairman of the Gravesend Historical Society. He was so impressed by what he learnt of the unit some years ago that as a hobby he researched as much as he could of what was officially code-named XD Operations carried out by the Kent Fortress Royal Engineers. At that time a number of the men who had taken part in the operations were still alive and he was able to interview them.

I would also like to thank the Royal Engineers Library for their loan of the notes by the late Major Bernard Buxton DSO. Alan Wakefield of the Imperial War Museum kindly undertook a search for any possible relevant photographs.

No official photographer accompanied the operations described here for reasons that will become obvious. Lance Corporal Hill, the HQ draughtsman in 1941, took on the role of Official War Artist and produced the drawings in this book from photographs taken by some of the officers and men and descriptions given to him by the participants.

This Territorial Army Unit was very much a family affair. In this relatively small industrial community everyone knew each other well, their backgrounds and families. My father was not only the largest employer locally, but he was Chairman of the local District Council and Chairman of the Bench. Because he had been extended in command of the Kent Fortress Royal Engineers no less than three times by 1939, he was very much a father figure in the hierarchy of the unit. The average age of all ranks was higher in the TA than their regular counterparts; on parade a number of them bore First Word War medals. My father was in his early fifties when these events took place.

In editing this book my task was made much easier by the fact that I knew many of the men in the original unit, some of them extremely well. I was in my early teens at the time and inevitably I was aware of some of the facts after the events had taken place. I joined the Army myself towards the end of the war and served for thirty odd years in the Royal Engineers.

Finally I am greatly indebted to my wife, Helen, who took on the task of correcting and typing this book.

P.H. (Jock) Brazier,
Marnhull, Dorset, October 2003

Chapter One

# PRELUDE TO ACTION

The beginning of the story was in those far off days, pre-war, pre-crises in fact, when as a Territorial Fortress Company Royal Engineers, we trained together with the Heavy Coast Defence gunners to resist sea borne attack upon the Thames River and estuary. With its endless docks and many miles of coastline, the numerous industries, together with its vital geographical situation in relation to the capital of the Empire, we certainly gained the impression that our responsibility was not to be taken lightly. Hence it was not considered at all surprising that during the crisis in the autumn of 1938, we were embodied and spread around our war stations in the estuary. This period lasted just a month, then back to factory and workshop again. When, a year later, after progressively menacing moves by Germany, war broke out, not only did mobilization cause little comment amongst the men, but the move to the forts seemed natural and inevitable. The wartime footing of the defences not only meant day and night watch-keeping in order that the searchlights could spring into action at a moments notice, but in addition to all the ordinary hum-drum activities of the garrison we were busy modernizing our equipment.

The convoy of buses moved off towards our war stations, all farewells were taken, and the sorrowing families left behind to turn over in their minds what it all meant. How long would it be, when would we return? Off we went, men and baggage lumbering through town and countryside and, as is the custom, singing heartily the songs of the people. It was a queer repertoire, telling of their affection for 'South of the Border', and all the oft repeated hit tunes of the dance halls and radio. A raucous mouth organ would lead them in quick succession from tune to tune but every now and again in the cycle, a particularly strident air would stir the tired ones, and bring them back to renewed vocal effort to proclaim in the most dominant manner, 'GOOD MORNING MR STEVENS AND WINDY NOTCHY KNIGHT'.

### Good morning, Mr Stevens and windy Notchy Knight

> *Hurrah for the CRE.*

> For we're working very hard down at Upnor Hard

> *Hurrah for the CRE.*
> *You make fast, I make fast, make fast the dinghy,*
> *Make fast the dinghy, make fast the dinghy,*
> *You make fast, I make fast, make fast the dinghy,*
> *Make fast the dinghy, pontoon*
> *For we're marching on to Laffan's Plain,*
> > *To Laffan's Plain, to Laffan's Plain,*
> *Yes, we're marching on to Laffan's Plain,*
> *Where they don't know mud from clay.*
> *Ah, Ah, Ah, Ah, Ah, Ah, Ah,*
> *Oshta, oshta, oshta, oshta.*
> *Ikona malee, piccanin skoff,*
> *Maninga sabenza, there's another off,*
> > *Oolum-da cried Matabele,*
> > *Oolum-da, away we go.*
> *Ah, Ah, Ah, Ah, Ah, Ah, Ah,*
> *Shuush . . . . . . . . . . . . Whoow!*

On this occasion I pondered over this oft repeated and familiar doggerel, and wondered what either of the worthies quoted did to merit such immortalization. It came back to Chatham from the Boer War. It is sung to the same refrain as 'We're marching on to Pretoria' and the fact remains that wherever sappers are gathered together (and the party isn't too dry!) the RE song is bound to break out sooner or later. On company concert programmes it is styled 'Hurrah for the CRE'! Moreover, I remembered an old gramophone record of it in the Sergeants' Mess and at dances it was sometimes played as a one-step. At times one would hear less complimentary and quite unprintable variations of the words of which it may be wise to say no more.

As we bumped along towards our destination, which was to mean such a tremendous upheaval in all our lives, I turned the peculiar insistence of these flippant verses over in my mind and was forced to the conclusion that the words did not matter, although the reference to Upnor Hard was apposite enough. What then was it that perpetuated it down the years? The tune might be considered invigorating, but could hardly be credited with much musical merit! By this process of *reductio ad absurdum* there was only one answer, it was the saga of the sapper, and that is all there is to the matter. Hence it has travelled to the four corners of the earth with the Corps motto, *Ubique*. I wondered, 'How far will these lads take this very peculiar song before they return to their homes for good?'

My reverie came to an abrupt end when the convoy pulled up beside the parade ground within the area of the fort, and the keen night air coming in from the sea quickly brought one back to realities. The all important duties of off-loading and distribution of manning details to action stations was the occupation of the moment.

During those early days, through the hard winter of 1939, all were keyed up by the expectation that great things were about to happen, and we should be in the stalls for the performance. Then, doubts crept in. Discussions and speculations in the mess and barracks had in the past centred around the type of attack we might reasonably expect – whether it would be a light raiding force of motor torpedo boats, or large block ships that would sink themselves in the fairway, or some kind of fleet action, with or without an attempt at invasion – but now we began to wonder whether it would come at all!

In the 'piping days of peace' there were night runs, when high speed craft would exercise their wiliest tactics to evade the penetrating beams of light. On they would come, twisting, turning and jinxing about in the inky blackness of night, at times wallowing stationary bow on in the hope that the beam would pass over unsuspecting, then the dash in through the black patches of unlighted water. Once in the beam they would be held and followed, meantime the guns would blaze away, round after round. The only lack of realism, so we thought then, was the blank ammunition, hence it was not surprising that when real war came, it was a bitter disappointment to find the encounter of our dreams existed solely in the imagination. The German High Seas Fleet could have joined Sweden in her neutral outlook for all we saw of them; an excellent thing from a national point of view, but it made life less interesting for us. As those long winter months crept by the truth became fairly obvious. Our job was remote from any action and, whatever chance there may have been, in the opening phases of hostilities, of an attack upon the port it now all seemed highly improbable. The inevitable reaction upon the minds of the men, all anxious to do their bit, can well be imagined, the slow developing feelings of frustration, disappointment and futility.

The old forts were laid out in regular angles to a geometric pattern with bastions and moats on principles dating from the great French engineer of former days, Vauban. There were the relics and remains of many generations of gunners where changes had been made with each succeeding improvement in armament. The glacis of earth, beyond the moat, must have been a task in keeping with the works of Ancient Egyptians. As the CRE (Commander Royal Engineers) I pondered on the geometry of the place and tried to visualize the fire plan of the original defenders of these shores.

These forts dating back into history, with their grim masonry walls, miserable little windows, and with the general air of mediaeval prisons, in themselves gave a background to the mental outlook of the garrison. The living accommodation was mainly old casemates with domed brick roofs covered again by many feet of earth and concrete and through the cracks the water trickled down the walls. With little or no ventilation, two courses remained open – either to have large fires and produce a kind of Turkish bath atmosphere, or alternatively to freeze in one's tomblike surroundings. In one case the fort was an island in the river, rather like a large lighthouse with the tide oozing in and out below the floor and adding its smell to the atmosphere inside. During the winter months it was perpetually dark inside and over the door was chalked 'abandon hope all who enter here'.

My room, like the others, had a vaulted roof and was just over the central archway leading in to the interior of the keep, the audible conversation of the guard below and all who went in and out, floated up to my open window. The unconscious humour of much of this and the references to our peculiar share in the war gave one food for thought. I, personally, was very well looked after by Corporal Holland, my batman. He was a very popular figure and I believe had been a professional boxer at one time. He was one of the few men in the unit who had not been an employee at Bevans Cement Works in Northfleet before the war. He was landlord of the King of the Belgiums public house on the river-front at Gravesend which he ran with his sister, as he was a bachelor.

In spite of all this, night after night these gunners and sappers kept their weary vigil, peering out into the inky blackness over the North Sea, frequently in the teeth of an east wind which overcame all efforts to keep warm by wrapping up. Speaking of wrapping up, the British soldier is a past master at this – starting with regulation issue clothing he adds several cardigans, arctic socks, mittens, gloves, balaclava helmet, plus an old oilskin which he puts on over his greatcoat, and gets a pal to rope him around the middle. Then fortified by a tot of rum he goes up to his OP gun site or emplacement for his watch, looking more like a bundle than a human being.

Not withstanding the discomforts, the troops were singularly good-natured about their new found mode of life which fate or Hitler had thrust upon them. They did all that was asked of them, behaved well and carried on; but always hoping against hope that something would turn up to relieve the monotony. Meanwhile the Hun was overrunning Poland with a thoroughness and frightfulness that proved all too well that the breed had not changed since the First World War. Quite a number of the older men had served in the last war, and would regale the younger members with tales, largely augmented by imagination no doubt, of the stirring events and bloody battles of those days, but always with a happy ending. It was inevitable that these men, who were volunteers and had given their leisure in peace to train as soldiers would feel that circumstances had cheated them and become, as the army so aptly puts it, 'browned off'. I can recall a scrap of conversation that sums the situation up fairly well.

The setting was a Company Office, the principal character the sergeant clerk, who was still smarting under a reprimand for some slip in procedure. Addressing himself to a younger NCO, he was heard to observe, 'I don't know chum, this war ain't like the last, ruddy good war that, plenty of fight and no fuss; this war, no fight but all ruddy fuss.'

Spasms of off duty were devoted to football, NAAFI concerts, and in the case of officers, sherry parties, but whilst this helped to entertain it did not relieve the ennui, for the simple reason that they did not want entertaining, they wanted to get on with the war.

This is a point of view frequently not appreciated by those well meaning people at the top always trying to organize entertainment for the troops which, while necessary, should be in small doses. The average soldier is quite keen to get on with his job, to learn more about his new found calling, to become more efficient, but above all to get on with the war.

We had an arrangement with the gunners that we would mount guard on alternate nights with them at the Quarter Guard leading into the Fort. This led to great rivalry between the Royal Regiment and the Corps; at first it took the form of competition in the matter of turn out with wholly beneficial results. Guard duty became an orgy of trouser pressing, polishing, and burnishing, until the respective excellence of guards RA and RE became a topic of conversation; not unnaturally, we thought ours the best. Looking round for new fields to conquer, commanders would practice the ritual of changing guards, until the precision of command and movement would have found favour with a grenadier. Then boredom set in, and the rivalry took an unfortunate turn, when the night sappers were on guard it was woe betide an erring gunner who, returning from the local hostelry, sought admission! One would see the eager NCO waiting anxiously to bang the heavy doors, breathlessly watching his wrist watch for the split second! The reverse process would take effect if it was a gunner night and a gentle tap on the outside would gain admission for those wearing a white lanyard. However a few fights outside were only symptomatic of the irritation of all this watching and waiting, for up in the town they stuck together when they met the sailors ashore. It was not the war they expected, it just seemed like another training period without end.

The cookhouse too, was another combined operation requiring much tact on the part of the orderly sergeant to convince the opposing teams that they each had a fair division. The story went round that a sapper who was aggrieved with the size of his dinner, produced the offending morsel in his mess tin to the orderly sergeant for inspection, only to be charged with having a dirty receptacle.

We sappers tried to preserve our keenness by building additional observation posts, emplacements and field fortifications during the day, in addition to our nightly watches – anything and, in fact, everything about the forts and their environs that needed improving, fell to our lot. This proved a blessing, but it seems strange to think that one could get mental uplift from erecting barbed wire entanglements on those frozen marshes and mud flats which fringe the coastline on the estuary, often working in half-light and invariably in foul weather. But it is a fact that it did us more good than all the entertainment. We really felt we were doing something besides the interminable watching and waiting. Even an occasional raid by the German sea planes which came over at night and laid mines, helped to revive enthusiasm. The ack-ack guns would put up a good display of tracer on these rare visits of the enemy, and our seaward searchlights had the fun of following them in, as far as elevation would permit. But the reaction soon set in, and the entire garrison again began to feel that they were in the remotest backwater of this very queer war. It will be remembered that in the spring of 1940 little land fighting took place so even news was scanty.

But we were wrong. By a peculiar combination of events many of us were, before long to have our share of the excitement. It

11

happened like this. An influx of additional troops to the coast defences, coupled with the fact that others were taking over the searchlights, resulted in our being transferred away from the forts, to Milton Barracks, Gravesend. We carried on our training in fieldworks, bridging, pontooning, and such like sapper activities. Long marches and exercises out in the country were a welcome relief to our previous existence and offered at least some hope of being drafted to an active theatre of war.

One day early in 1940, before the other units had joined us, a Senior Officer came down and inspected us at work; at the time we were training in demolitions. He asked whether we could take over certain highly secret responsibilities, from another formation that was under orders for France. I jumped at the prospect and before long found myself before a small staff committee unfolding the plan and outlining requirements. This was during the time of the nine months phoney war after the Germans had invaded Poland. The military planners realized that should they strike at France, they would almost certainly adopt the strategy of the First World War and achieve a flanking movement by invading the Low Countries. This was the famous *Schliefen* plan adopted in 1914. Should this happen and if they invaded both Holland and Belgium, the Allies would move into Belgium to confront them. However the North Sea ports would almost inevitably fall into enemy hands. In this war very large oil stocks were held at Amsterdam, Rotterdam and Antwerp and it was known that the Germans were desperately short of fuel oil of all grades. The proposal was that our unit would be called on to provide small demolition teams to go, under Admiralty command, to land and destroy these very important oil stocks if the Germans invaded.

It was a thrilling opportunity to really get cracking, as the sappers say, but there was a snag. Nothing could be done unless the Germans invaded the Low Countries. Weeks went by, and perversely enough it did not happen; all the same we had hope and something to encourage us. The next few weeks were spent in harder and tougher training. As may be imagined, speculation amongst the men was rife as to their ultimate objective, perhaps the most popular idea was the invasion of Heligoland. At night two or three officers, who had been let into the secret would meet behind locked doors and study plans, maps, charts of waterways and aerial photographs, making detailed plans for personnel, explosives and other equipment. There was no precedent for demolition on anything like this scale, therefore a number of different options were considered on methods of destruction which could be employed to destroy oil storage tanks with the limited stores that the small parties of men would be able to carry. (For details see Appendix III)

Unarmed combat was not heard of so much in those days, but we developed movement by night, practised stealth and studied quiet methods of liquidating sentries without alarming the neighbourhood. We visited certain industrial plants, docks and quays that may have put Heligoland into the men's minds. Because of the secrecy of the proposed operations it was impossible to carry out any specific training that would suggest the destruction of bulk oil installations. Looking back on those days one is impressed with the tonic effect upon all ranks of some definite objective. Perhaps the most significant aspect is how the dullest existence can become brimful of interest by an unexpected twist of fate. The difficulty is to get men who, in long periods of training and waiting, are living in a state of suspended animation to realize that their turn may be close at hand.

Looking back, those periods in life that seemed so dull, in reality passed quickly enough, although at the time they seemed interminable. Similarly, the minor irritations and disappointments of life assume their correct perspective and sink into insignificance against the background of memory. In fact there is quite a lot of amusement to be gained in reflection upon the anxiety to be doing something different, or our impetuousness for time to pass quickly. It passes all too quickly as we came to discover.

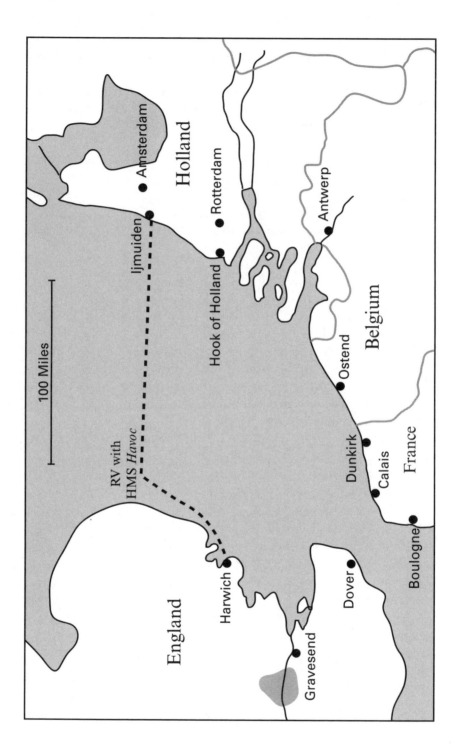

Chapter Two

# ACTION STATIONS –
# AMSTERDAM

During the early part of the year 1940 the German Army had been massing troops along the Dutch frontier and there was a long drawn out period of tension. At this time the Dutch had taken what they considered to be adequate counter-measures by preparing bridges for demolition and flooding tracts of their country in the hope that this would deter or harass the threatening enemy just over the frontier. At the same time they maintained strict neutrality and appeared to assume a rather lofty detachment from the march of events. It must be remembered that Holland had not engaged in any war for over 100 years and, no doubt, clung to the hope that Germany would respect her neutrality. The forces at her disposal were pathetically poorly equipped and trained compared with her powerful neighbour but in spite of this she refused cooperation with the Allies until it was too late to be effective. It was fairly obvious to the observer that the mechanized enemy might, and probably would, overrun the country and that at best the Dutch could only fight a delaying action.

It so happened that large petrol refineries and oil stocks existed at Amsterdam and Rotterdam which, bearing in mind the enemy's great need for these products for his army and air force, consti- tuted a very tempting prize quite apart from the other resources of the country. This did not escape the notice of our Government. The direct result was that when, in the early hours of 10 May Hitler gave his army orders to invade Holland, three small parties of our formation, who had been at two hours' notice to move for

15

several days, moved to Dover within the hour to join a naval operation designed to cope with the situation. It must be appreciated that at this time in the war there was no Combined Operations HQ and so these operations were all carried out under Naval Command. On shore the joint naval and sapper demolition parties were, in each case, commanded by a Naval Commander, RN, not to be confused with the skippers of the destroyers. The parties moved down to Dover in specially requisitioned lorries. One of the lorries broke down on the way and they were forced to waylay a passing lorry carrying a large quantity of gas bottles. When they arrived alongside the destroyer these gas bottles were inadvertently cross-loaded onto the ship as the Navy thought they were part of the sappers' demolition equipment. These had to be returned to the quay and the hapless driver was faced with reloading them himself.

At eleven o'clock HM destroyers *Whitshead*, *Wild Swan*, *Verity* and *Brilliant* left harbour at full speed. The plan was for the leading vessel, *Whitshead* to make for Ijmuiden carrying the sapper party for Amsterdam, the second, *Wild Swan* to go to the Hook of Holland with Rotterdam as the sapper objective, the third, *Verity* to Flushing with no sapper party as there were no significant oil stocks there and finally, *Brilliant* would try to get up the Scheldt as far as possible and put a party off for Antwerp. Because the position at the latter port was very much the same as the Dutch ports as regards oil stocks and installations, it was included in this operation.

*Whitshead* had on board a naval demolition party of eighty men to destroy the port facilities at Ijmuiden and eighteen NCOs and men of the Royal Engineers demolition party under Captain Peter Keeble and his second-in-command Lieutenant Don Terry, to deal with the oil installations at Amsterdam. Both the naval and sapper demolition parties were under command of Commander Goodenough RN. Besides the 100-odd extra personnel who were additional to the destroyer's normal complement, cases of explosives, arms, ammunition and equipment were piled on all available deck space until there was hardly standing room. The ship's company were grand hosts, as the Royal Navy always are, and in spite of the choppy sea that raked the destroyers from stem to stern, the demolition parties were in high spirits.

It was at this stage that Keeble, the OC of the sapper detachment could break silence and brief the men on their objectives in general. He told them that the sappers, on reaching Ijmuiden, would move on to Amsterdam and destroy the vast oil stocks located in tank farms. In addition he distributed Dutch money which had been provided to buy food as there were no such things as twenty-four-hour individual ration packs or similar emergency food supplies at the beginning of the war. It was hoped that it would also assist them generally when ashore. As to their method of withdrawal, he could not be too reassuring. The navy would do their best to take them off but the safety of HM Destroyers was of paramount importance and the captains were ordered not to hazard their ships unnecessarily in order to evacuate what were, after all, only a handful of soldiers. In short, there was no guaranteed return ticket for the sappers.

Nearing the Dutch coast, *Whitshead* was the first to be attacked by a lone German bomber but it was driven off by the ship's guns. The captain took avoiding action, zigzagging violently at full speed. Port and starboard gunwales were alternately awash and life for those on deck was a misery. Attacks by several aircraft developed later on and eventually after several near misses, *Whitshead* was hit on the port side aft, killing and wounding several ratings and blowing half a dozen more men into the sea. The sapper demolition party were lucky not to suffer any casualties. It also set fire to some cordite in the ammunition locker on deck. It hardly needs saying what a devastating effect it would have had if it had spread to the explosives stored on deck. The fire was quickly dealt with by some sailors who, with great bravery, seized the cordite boxes and threw them overboard. The ship went round in a circle to pick up the men but was again heavily attacked from the air and the skipper could do no more than throw over Carley floats for them before racing on to Ijmuiden. Lance Corporal Twocock's account after the operation sums it up:

*4.30 p.m. enemy planes sited – bombed from a great height – replied with AA guns.*

*Began to realize we were a suicide squad. Everyone was gay and it seemed like a pleasure trip.*

*5 p.m. Rum Issue – corned beef sandwiches and tea. Nearing the Dutch coast and expecting trouble any minute. More planes over-head and things began to fly – all guns were manned and we took cover. Had those sailors got <u>guts</u>! We could hear the whistle of the bombs as they hit the water – two port side and one aft. We had a marvellous skipper – the ship was doing . . . knots and twisting and turning like an eel. All we could do was hang on and pray.*

*Captain Keeble and Vic Huggett were lying beside me when a terrific crash occurred and the ship lifted clear out of the water. The bomb ignited some cordite and it was burning on deck near the ammunition. One sailor grabbed an armful and threw it overboard. Another grabbed the rest and jumped over with it.*

At about 6 p.m. *Whitshead* reached the entrance to Ijmuiden harbour. The destroyer's attempts to come alongside were being frustrated by air attacks. However, on the fourth attempt she made it. The parties and the stores were unloaded rapidly under further continual but fortunately ineffective air attack. As soon as this was completed *Whitshead* slipped her moorings and put to sea again.

As Amsterdam is the best part of twenty miles inland from Ijmuiden, Commander Goodenough had arranged for a 'one coach special' train to take them there. He was very concerned at how exposed the sapper party would be because of the news of the rapid German advance and therefore he detached a young naval officer and sixteen blue jackets to assist as a covering party and placed them under Captain Keeble's command.

When they arrived at Amsterdam railway station they were greeted by crowds cheering their 'British Allies' who had come, they thought, to defend their country. Fortunately they did not appreciate their real intention. The situation they found was already far graver than had been generally realized. The Dutch Naval Officer representing the C.-in-C. Amsterdam wished them to go to the local Naval Barracks. Keeble was appalled as he was more than anxious to go straight to his objectives and start preparing them for demolition. At the back of his mind were his instructions 'that at all costs the oil must not fall into enemy hands'. He left the men in the station café temporarily and went with the young British naval officer to find the British Consulate.

Although the Consul General was trying to be helpful he was unable to get any response out of The Hague so, for the moment there was no alternative but to accept the Dutch hospitality and stay the night in the Naval Barracks. This rather dashed the sappers' enthusiasm as they had hoped to be at their task of blowing up the oil tanks in about half an hour!

They passed a restless night in the barracks with frequent air raids which were getting heavier and heavier. At 8 a.m. the Vice Consul arrived and took Keeble away for what they called staff talks with the Dutch authorities. Keeble returned in the afternoon after having seen the Dutch Commander-in-Chief, in person, who had been told by The Hague that the British sappers, were to be under his command and that they had come for the express purpose of preparing the oil stocks for demolition. Keeble had also managed to visit all the installations, meet managers and get information of the layout of the plants and type of oil stored without giving too much away as to his real intention. He appreciated that if they thought he was going to destroy their oil they would all be up in arms. He hoped that he had given the impression that they were going to protect the installations from German parachutists.

Armed with the valuable information gained, the next consideration was to get the men together with their explosives, arms and other equipment, distribute them over the three installations and to make a plan for the demolitions. Obviously the first problem was transport. Keeble interviewed the Dutch again, and, without speaking a word of the language, succeeded by pencil and paper and hastily drawn sketches to convince them that in the first place the enemy would get these valuable fuel supplies unless they acted quickly and also that our party could and would prevent this and finally, that the part the Dutch had to play was to be helpful and provide transport. A fairly heavy strafing from the air at the time stimulated the official mind to the extent that the sappers were allowed to requisition, solemnly and with all necessary documentation, three motor launches.

At dusk the same evening a greatly relieved Captain Keeble had the satisfaction of moving his small force consisting of two officers and eighteen NCOs and men to their objectives. He allocated the party to their respective tasks, at the same time giving verbal orders outlining his plan including withdrawal routes and rendezvous (RVs). A signal for action was arranged for firing the tank farms but stressing the fact that, come what may, they should not allow the plants to fall into German hands.

During the night they crept about the plants making a more detailed survey of the contents of the scores of large tanks and the main layout of the extensive pipelines and the pumping arrangements.

It must be remembered that this operation started when they landed at Ijmuiden on Friday evening and it was now Sunday morning. It had been impossible to buy food as the shops were shut over the weekend and the country was being invaded and subject to incessant air attack. The sappers were desperately short of food and a foraging party set off and shortly met a group of Dutch sailors. They asked if any of them spoke English and to their amazement one said that he did and abandoned his colleagues to join the small group of sappers. He said ' Come with me' and led them back to the Dutch Naval Barracks. He told them that everyone in the barracks would take cover when the next air raid started and this would be their opportunity. They did not have long to wait, a raid started and predictably all personnel evacuated buildings and took cover. After a suitable pause he boldly entered the cookhouse and returned a few minutes later with a large bucket of food. Their new found friend remained with them until their final withdrawal and proved invaluable.

At this time things began to look bad in Holland. Although it was impossible to get a reliable picture of the actual position, it was freely rumoured that the Germans were advancing towards the coast and that the Dutch resistance, whilst stubborn in places, was by no means consistent. Aerial attacks met with practically no opposition. Some of the population appeared to have a friendly feeling towards the invader for one reason or another, and sniping was not uncommon, which seemed to indicate that the end was not far off. At one stage the Dutch Naval C.-in-C. under whose command they were, tried to get the sappers to return to the Naval

Barracks as he feared that they might fire the oil without his permission. Keeble rightly resisted this order as he said that the position was so precarious that the men must stay where they were. During this period the sappers did much useful preparation and despite the small naval covering party still had to stay alert and be on their guard all the time.

Early on the Monday morning, 13 May, Goodenough contacted Keeble by phone and told him to carry out all demolitions at once but to try and phone The Hague as a courtesy on a specific number he was given but even if agreement wasn't forthcoming, to 'blow' anyhow. In the event Keeble got straight through to The Hague and a very agitated voice said 'do it now' and repeated 'do it now'. It sounded as though he was then torn from the phone.

The order to fire was transmitted by Keeble mainly by using the refineries' private telephone systems. They exclusively adopted the system of blowing off the cocks to the tanks with gun cotton to flood the areas between the tanks and the bunds. When they fired Very light cartridges into the air over the bunds the fuel would ignite and burn furiously about fifty foot above the pool of petrol. This phenomenon was caused by lack of sufficient oxygen until it reached this height. Eventually, with an enormous whoomph a whole tank would take off into the air, roll over and fall down. This tickled the sappers' imagination no end! The flames grew higher and higher and the black smoke denser and denser. The flames eventually reached several hundred feet and the smoke drifted slowly over the city. At each installation the firing of the oil tanks started down wind and they then slowly worked their way upwind attacking other targets. When a tank or group of tanks contained only heavy fuel oil, blankets were brought out and soaked in kerosene as planned and used to ignite the heavy fuel oil behind the bunds. This method had to be watched for ten or fifteen minutes to ensure ignition was taking place. It was noticed that when the heavy oil or bunker fuel had become sufficiently warm wisps of smoke would appear showing that the fuel had started to vaporize and they knew then that the fire would take hold shortly.

After the destruction of the outlying tank farms was completed the sappers made their way back to the RV at Petroleum Haven, the largest of the installations, where Keeble was waiting to fire the last lot of storage tanks. When this was done they were ready to pull out. The spectacle of a large oil plant wholly on fire is a sight not easily forgotten. It must be borne in mind that all this was achieved by a tiny group of sappers and sailors in the face of the invading German army.

The three launches that they had at their disposal were provided primarily for withdrawal down the canal system to Ijmuiden. However Keeble had been warned that the Germans had laid mines from the air in the canals to paralyse all movement. Keeble had taken the precautionary measure of sending two sappers out on to the main road to seize the first decent sized lorry they saw and hold it for their eventual withdrawal to the coast. At this stage they all climbed onto the lorry including their 'tame' Dutch sailor and drove fast towards Ijmuiden. They came across a number of roadblocks that they crashed through at speed, their lorry bristling with rifles, and eventually arrived safely at the port. At this point Keeble met Commander Goodenough again and returned his covering party of sailors with thanks. It was always intended that once the sappers had destroyed the oil they would assist the small naval party in destroying the port infrastructure. Lieutenant Don Terry went with about half a dozen sappers round one side of the docks to help the Navy and Keeble with about a dozen men to the other side. Keeble had appreciated as soon as they arrived, that with the destroyer long gone, the prospect of evacuation did not appear too good and therefore looked round for a small ship or boat to use to get away. Eventually he found a motor boat about thirty-two foot long and he placed two of his sappers and the Dutch sailor on it as a precautionary measure to guard it. The latter was still anxious to stick with them and had obtained from somewhere a small wireless transmitter that he claimed he could work.

Lock gates, cranes, a floating dock and coast defences went up one after another and finally the sinking of two block ships left the heavy mark of the Navy assisted by sappers, on this port.

An hour or so after their arrival they saw the party under Terry leaving in a small tug from the other side of the harbour. This tug met up with a small coaster when out at sea which they boarded and persuaded a reluctant skipper to sail for England. Eventually, whether through incompetence or not wishing to comply with their orders it became apparent that they were hopelessly lost in the North Sea. Fortunately they came across a British destroyer onto which they clambered and arrived safely back at Dover in due course.

When Keeble's party had finished their remaining demolition tasks, it was quite late in the evening and approaching dusk. As there was no sign of a destroyer standing off to take them aboard they felt there was no alternative but to board the open motor-boat that they had been holding for this eventuality and head out to sea. The boat had no navigational instruments or charts on board but did have a compass. The one thing they knew was that England lay to their west and they motored due west assuming that they must ultimately make a landfall should they not be picked up before.

They left Ijmuiden just before dusk and were repeatedly attacked by enemy fighters. The sappers had only rifles to defend themselves. Small arms fire from only twelve men sitting and standing in a small boat in a seaway was not likely to be very effective! They circled round several times and Keeble realized that as it was getting darker, the flashes from their rifle fire were probably giving their position away. He ordered them to cease firing and his hunch paid off as the enemy lost them in the darkness. All that night and through the next day they headed slowly due west. Fortunately the sea was calm. By now they were extremely tired and hungry as they hadn't had a proper meal or nights sleep for some days. On the second night out the Dutchman claimed that he was in touch with a British destroyer on his small transmitter. Keeble said to him 'I will believe you when I see it'. As you can imagine, they were getting pretty desperate now but sure enough an hour or two later, out of the dark the destroyer HMS *Havoc* appeared, on passage from Norway to Harwich. With hindsight it was thought that Admiral Ramsay, in charge at Dover had probably sent out a signal to all HM ships asking them to keep a look out for parties of soldiers in small boats trying to get back to England. It was an amazing RV, as in those days there was no shipborne radar and the Navy at that time, did not have efficient

Direction Finding equipment. *Havoc*, still showing her battle scars, was a household name at the time having just taken part with the other H class destroyers in the first Battle of Narvik.

The Captain shouted at them through a loud hailer to climb on board without delay and in the same breath congratulated them on having just crossed one of our minefields. Now, an extraordinary thing happened. The Dutch sailor who had been with them through so much, was suddenly overcome with emotion and felt that he must return to Holland. This was the last that was seen of him and no one knows whether he made it back alone or what became of him. Once the sappers were aboard the Master-at-Arms collected all their weapons for safe storage. The Navy, as always, were most generous hosts although really all the men wanted to do was get a bite to eat and a good sleep. When they reached Harwich, Keeble had a slight altercation with the captain of *Havoc*. It must be pointed out that because of the special nature of these sapper operations, a considerable number of the men had been issued with .38 revolvers as well as their rifles. The former were in exceedingly short supply at this time in the war. It was these that the captain was more than reluctant to part with. However Keeble stood his ground and refused to allow his soldiers to disembark until they were returned!

They were safely disembarked at the naval shore establishment at Harwich where every comfort was provided so they were able to shave, clean themselves up and were given a hearty breakfast. A senior naval officer who was obviously aware of the role they had played came and congratulated them. In due course they returned by train to their base at Gravesend and despite everything they had accomplished and endured, like good soldiers they still had all their weapons.

Chapter Three

# ROTTERDAM

The sapper party for the Rotterdam refineries and oil stocks was under the command of Captain Tommy Goodwin with three of the recently joined second lieutenants and about forty men from the unit.

On the outward voyage the second destroyer, *Wild Swan*, parted company with the leader in the North Sea and when opposite the Hook of Holland, headed inshore. This too had its share of attention from the German aircraft that were sweeping up and down the Dutch coast at that time. It almost looked as if the enemy were expecting Britain to aid the Dutch forces with a landing, and were determined to take a heavy toll. The combined naval and sapper party under command of Commander Hill RN, arrived at the Hook of Holland at 4.30 p.m. only to find, like the Amsterdam party, that no arrangements had been made for them, nor indeed, was the nature of their mission understood by the authorities ashore. The Naval Commander, after consultation with our naval attaché, decided that the sappers had better get on towards their objectives in Rotterdam, where they were, if possible, to contact a responsible Dutch authority. In any case they were to prevent the considerable fuel stocks falling into enemy hands. Just as the Naval Commander and sapper officers were about to set off in a launch up the River Maas a further hitch occurred, which savoured of the Arabian Nights. A signal had been received that between thirty and forty tons of gold was still in the bank at Rotterdam and that every effort was to be made to get it away. As a side show to the main job this caused some surprise and amusement; after all, humping tons of gold does not often fall to the lot of the ordinary soldier. As a result Commander Hill decided to accompany the two sapper officers to Rotterdam and they proceeded up the river by pilot boat.

Captain Goodwin and Second Lieutenant Paul Baker landed at Lekhaven at 11 p.m. and in the darkness made their way ashore into the town with the idea of finding some government official. This they certainly managed to do, but not quite in the manner they had hoped, for they soon found themselves arrested and detained in a military post commanded by an elderly Dutch captain.

The Germans were approaching and a good deal of that inevitable confusion that is born of rumour was current in the city. It certainly looked as if they would end their days in a concentration camp, or perhaps as prisoners working in a German coal mine. Tommy Goodwin was a South African and, in the hope of improving the situation by convincing the guards that he was on their side, he tried them with a high flown appeal in Afrikaans. The result was disastrous, as they could neither understand him nor did they believe that they were English; their situation now seemed fairly hopeless. So far they had resisted being disarmed in spite of fairly heated demands by their captors. When for a moment all the guards but one withdrew from the room and Goodwin was on the point of trying to shoot his way out, Commander Hill was brought in also under arrest.

In time Hill and Goodwin persuaded the Dutch captain that they were all British Allies and asked to be put in touch with the bank officials, and also a director of one of the largest oil plants. So the time spent under arrest was far from wasted, and was eventually turned to great advantage. After having drunk each other's health, several times, and sworn eternal friendship with the appropriate toast of damnation to the Hun, at least that is what it seemed to be, judging by the manner in which it was received by all present, the three British officers parted company with their captors. The naval officer went off to negotiate the release of the bullion with the bank and government officials.

Released from imprisonment, the sapper officers went about the task of reconnaissance and meeting the various directors. The Dutch authorities would not agree to an immediate occupation by our troops. Crossing over to the south side and landing at one of the installations Goodwin found the place deserted except for German patrols, as by now, the Germans were in occupation of much of the south side of the river. The presence of enemy troops in the vicinity of the plants before the actual fall of Rotterdam came as a surprise. After having taken a cautious look round, with one eye on a strolling sentry, Goodwin decided to re-cross the river and make further efforts to get in touch with the Dutch Military Commander or one of his deputies. This he did by telephone and explained the seriousness of the situation, but the Dutch general flatly refused to allow any demolition to be carried out, or even prepared. To make sure of it he gave instructions that the British officers were to be escorted back to the Hook. At about this time street fighting had broken out in Hudson Street near Lekhaven jetty which appeared to have been recently occupied by a small force of Germans. This was fortunate, because instead of escorting our young South African and his colleague back to the Hook, the Dutch invited them to join in the mêlée on their side. This no doubt appealed to them as an attractive diversion but with great self-control Goodwin decided that it would not help much with the job in hand. However, it gave them the chance to slip away unobserved and allowed them to make their way back to the Hook. They arrived back at 6 p.m. on Saturday after a fairly chequered and eventful journey and rejoined the rest of the sappers. Seeing that there was a destroyer lying alongside, perhaps waiting for the Dutch Royal Family, Tommy Goodwin thought it was a good opportunity to nip on board and have a bath. At the time the crew were all at action stations with the gun crews closed up as they were in a hazardous position. What Goodwin did not realize was that he was bathing directly under one of the after 4.7inch guns and also that German aircraft were approaching. Halfway through his bath there was an appalling crash as the gun opened fire, a basin fell to the deck and shattered and Tommy, thinking the ship must be sinking, ran out onto the top deck completely naked much to the amusement of the crew.

The Hook of Holland had been subject to fairly constant bombing while he had been away and considerable damage was done but the party had escaped casualties. This was really remarkable because there was literally no cover, and one had to rely on spreading out round the area and taking cover in the bomb craters.

On Sunday things became even worse and it was apparent that the end could not be far off. At this stage an official in the Dutch Government ordered immediate demolition of the fuel stocks. This resulted in the whole party of sappers going back to Rotterdam accompanied by a Dutch officer. Things really looked as if they were moving now, having at least some sort of official backing. On the contrary, when they arrived at Rotterdam they were met by a messenger who gave the Dutch officer written instructions forbidding them to do anything! Goodwin, by now heartily sick of the constant atmosphere of shilly shallying, struck off with his party towards the installations, determined to act on his own initiative and to see the job through in spite of official hindrance. Just as they got near the Schiehaven jetty a wave of low-level bombers flew over and dropped eighteen HE bombs, completely flattening the buildings and scattering the party. Fortunately the attack missed both the men and their explosives, which they were carrying on ordinary ambulance stretchers. As it was getting dark they took cover in a nearby deserted building which had evidently been a schoolroom. The raids on the town spread great havoc and confusion throughout the night, so there was no question of sleep, neither was there anything they could do at the time.

On Monday morning, with the first streaks of light, the party crept out and gazed upon the very smoky and battered area all round them. Goodwin received final instructions to blow the Shell plant, also the American Petroleum installations that were both on the south bank of the Maas. The directive also stated that on no account were the plants on the north bank to be destroyed as these contained mainly vegetable oils for food (margarine) which must be preserved at all costs. Faced with the opportunity at least of being able to get on with the job, a detachment moved off towards the plants via Vlaadingen and crossed the river. Goodwin interviewed the manager who, of course, protested with great vehemence. He gave him a signed statement, written in his presence, to the effect that he and his staff should withdraw at

28

once as it was his intention to blow the place up and fire the stocks, there and then.

The actual refinery was very large and modern and inevitably they only had a minimum of explosives which they had carried on medical stretchers. Goodwin ordered the men to destroy as much of the plant in the refinery with sledge hammers and thereafter they managed to flood the buildings with oil from a nearby tank which was subsequently ignited hoping to cause the maximum amount of damage to the plant by fire. They then turned their attention to the tank farm where, in general, they used the preferred method of demolition by blowing off the main cocks on the tanks with gun cotton, flooding inside the bund and then firing it. Goodwin had an interesting moment when standing within the bund of a tank. Baker, not realizing that he was there, decided to hole the tank with an anti-tank rifle. One assumes that Tommy Goodwin's words were unprintable! They then turned their attention to the American Petroleum installation and repeated the whole performance.

Corporal Blake's eyewitness account of these days, while waiting to be called forward from the Hook, and his memories of the actual demolition make interesting reading:

*We landed on Hook from destroyer, HMS Wild Swan on Friday, 10 May, 1940, under air attack. We soon experienced small arms fire and machine gun fire from German Paratroops and aircraft and German troops in the vicinity of the outskirts of the town. Fires began in the docks area and on railway trucks, etc. Our troops removed some burning trucks away from area.*

*At times some of us joined Dutch soldiers and marines manning trenches and positions in buildings about one mile out from our area. No evidence of any firing returned by our own chaps, although we came under fire from both Germans and Dutch. Only a few of us were involved in these exchanges; we received orders to return to our own position, then witnessed fire from destroyer against German positions.*

*Used Dutch lorries with their soldiers and drivers to check surrounding area for enemy location and for our demolition work, turned back after coming under fire a couple of times.*

*Saturday, Royal marines landed from a destroyer as a covering force for RN demolition parties, who prepared destruction of docks, rail installations, etc.*

*Sunday, detachment (Company) of Irish Guards landed from another destroyer, a bridgehead force to cover evacuation of Dutch Royal family.*

*Sometime during the first day or two a group of Blenheim fighter bombers came over – believe all were shot down in air battles with Germans.*

*At night – believe Sunday – most of us went aboard a ship and, keeping under cover, arrived at Rotterdam. Set to work demolishing oil and petrol storage tanks, breaking valves and pipes and blowing holes in tanks, started fires, sometimes with a fire of blankets soaked in kerosene, sometimes by firing tracer or Very light shells into the petrol, causing great fire and explosions. There was one incident of some of our chaps trying to cross to an island or promontory upon which were storage tanks, Germans were on there and opened fire. Someone had the idea to fire at tanks with anti-tank rifles, making holes – out poured the petrol, then we fired tracer across – terrific explosions, fires and destruction – up went the lot, enemy too.*

*All the time we provided our own cover, all Royal Engineers.*

By this time Commander Hill had at last been invited to remove the gold bullion, and the sappers, having completed their demolition task, turned to help. They loaded the bullion into vans that had already been provided and escorted them to Lekhaven jetty where it was loaded onto the pilot boat. This was all done during heavy air raids and nearby street fighting. The amusement and banter amongst the men while handling the heavy cases of solid gold would make a story in itself. Thirty-six tons were put aboard the pilot boat. Commander Hill, with some naval ratings, pushed off from the quay and with cheery farewells headed down river with the intention of joining the destroyer at the Hook. By a stroke of ill luck during the voyage they were blown up by a magnetic mine and all perished, leaving no trace of the men, gold or boat. Apart from the sad loss of a fine officer and the naval ratings, many millions of pounds worth of precious metal went to the bottom and added yet another item to the long list of treasure ships in Davy Jones's locker.

By this time the whole city seemed to be either in the process of being dive-bombed or indulging in street fighting. The terrible and vindictive onslaught that was inflicted on Rotterdam by the enemy is a matter of history now, but all the party agreed that it was a terrifying ordeal for the unfortunate population. It seemed as if the place was devoid of defences and the scene was one of stark horror, pure and simple. It was naturally with some relief, when the plants and buildings were blown up and fired, that the party withdrew by launch downriver to Vlaadingen. The flames were, by then, several hundred feet high and lit up the whole city with a bright glow, like some gigantic stage on which the tragedy of death and destruction was in full swing. When the party reached Vlaadingen, they transferred to the lorries which they had previously commandeered and were just about to set off, down the road towards the Hook, when they were informed by a Dutch officer who spoke English and wore a worried look, that numerous parachutists had dropped all along the route. They were mainly in the houses and farms on each side of the road and were holding up all movement between the Hook and Rotterdam. This seemed a serious predicament because any kind of detour was well nigh impossible, due to the intricate criss-cross pattern of waterways and drainage channels in the surrounding country.

Clearly, something had to be done, and done quickly, unless they were to be captured. They decided to test the truth of the Dutch officer's statement and to find out the enemy's strength. Accordingly they divided into two streams, one each side of the road, and skirmished from cover to cover and house to house, a small rear guard following up behind with the transport. Apart from an occasional burst of fire from the odd farm, which might just as well have been fired in the belief that the party were Huns, they made good progress.

They arrived back at the Hook at eight o'clock in the evening by which time the whole place was a complete shambles from aerial bombardment. They found the destroyer had put to sea with the Legation Staff earlier in the day which was a bit depressing, but being really tired they got under the remains of a string of wrecked railway wagons and slept through the night.

On the following day, forced by hunger and thirst, the party went on a scrounging expedition with such success that a really

31

high class breakfast was provided consisting of cocoa from a small Dutch naval vessel, stale bread from local ruins, fried chicken and duck from – well, it does not matter much where they came from. The remains of the local police post provided cigars to complete the feast and life seemed tolerably comfortable, except for the rather disturbing thought that there was no destroyer to take them back to England.

The officers in the party held a council of war, and decided that rather than face certain capture by the enemy, they would take possession of a small vessel at dusk and sail westwards. The scheme seemed simple enough and full of promise, until their coveted little vessel set sail on her own account, as indeed had the bulk of the shipping around the coast. Back again to where they were as regards escape, Goodwin had a chance meeting with a naval officer at the port, who told him that one of our destroyers was standing off outside and was shortly coming in for stragglers.

When the destroyer arrived, Goodwin asked the captain to send a message saying that they had destroyed 400,000 tons of oil on the south side of the river but the Dutch authorities refused to let them tackle the plant which had the vegetable oil on the north bank. At 13:00 hours he was given implicit instructions to withdraw immediately.

In the early afternoon the destroyer *Malcolm* came alongside, our party boarded her and, in company with another destroyer, set course for Dover. The second vessel which followed, while still off the Dutch coast, was repeatedly bombed and sustained casualties. By luck, the destroyer carrying the sappers was not attacked, and arrived back in Dover at midnight. The members of the Rotterdam raid stepped ashore, unshaven, with their clothes soaked in petrol and thoroughly grimy. They slept at a naval establishment that first night and, having cleaned themselves up and now presenting a tolerably human appearance, returned to their unit at Gravesend little if any the worse for several eventful days crowded with stirring memories, having witnessed the fall and destruction of Rotterdam.

Once again, although they had had to abandon some of their stores, they returned with all their weapons and remaining ammunition intact.

Chapter Four

# ANTWERP

The last of the four destroyers in line when they left Dover, HMS *Brilliant* was the first to break away; when abreast of Flushing she turned to starboard and entered the River Scheldt, pushing on upstream with the intention of getting as close to Antwerp as possible. The demolition party consisted of Second Lieutenant 'Shorty' Wells, one of the newly joined young officers from OCTU, in command of about sixteen men. The passage was strange as they passed craft of every description, all moving seawards in the hope of escaping damage or capture by the threatening hordes outside the city. Liners, tugs, large freighters, launches, tankers and the ubiquitous tramp steamers, their decks often tightly packed with refugees, were all making their way down to the sea, and freedom.

The destroyer, with the naval and sapper demolition parties on board, threaded her way through this avalanche of miscellaneous craft, round the bends of the Scheldt and right up to Antwerp, the one large and flourishing port of Belgium. The town itself, lying on the east side of the river, which flows north – south at that point, spreads out to form an imposing skyline with the cathedral towers prominent among the many fine buildings and wide expanse of humbler dwellings. For some miles the waterfront is flanked with docks, shipyards, offices, factories and all the evidence of a highly industrious people and thriving commercial enterprise. Ships from the Seven Seas were lying in the approaches to this busy port.

The destroyer anchored in the river, just off the pilots' head-quarters at the seaward end of the docks. The senior officers went ashore to visit the British Consul, whose offices were literally besieged with all classes of people desperate to secure passage to England. Belgian wives of Englishmen gesticulated at the harassed clerks, while their daughters wept as if to add poignancy to their mothers' appeal. Businessmen pressed their claim with a vigour and persuasiveness acquired in the hard school of commerce. At one side stood a tall and dignified white-haired old lady waiting for an interview with one of those overworked young officials. She was clearly English and amidst the entire hubbub had an air of quiet composure.

The naval and sapper demolition parties remained on board *Brilliant* in Antwerp for forty-eight hours, while the Naval Commander in charge, tried to negotiate for the two parties to be allowed to at least make a reconnaissance of their objectives. They were disembarked onto two tugs, one carrying naval personnel and the other the sappers. *Brilliant* then took on about eighty consular staff and others and sailed for home.

On all these operations it was laid down by the naval authori-ties that the 'Safety of HM ships was of paramount importance'. Thus not only was the expedition expected to cope with the situ-ation ashore and carry out their task, but also had to make their own way home without naval assistance. All were trained to act on their own initiative if separated or marooned and during the course of these operations they developed quite a remarkable homing instinct, so much so, that they invariably returned safely. One never quite knew when or how they would get back, but after some days they would report back to the unit's depot with as little concern as if returning from leave. This homing instinct, once developed, is largely a matter of common sense plus determina-tion, and the British soldier has frequently demonstrated his ability to get back, in the face of heavy odds and in spite of the efforts of the Germans to prevent it.

Air raids became fairly frequent. One unlucky ship packed with refugees received a direct hit and had to be beached to allow some

34

of the unfortunates to get ashore. As the tugs steamed across the river, they passed the city on the port side, and the Tête de Flandre on the other side on which stands one of those old forts, part of a ring of defences round the city. Standing like a ghost of some former military genius, it seemed to bear testimony to man's determination to safeguard his possessions against spoliation. With their bastion defences, ravelins, counter guards and retrenchments, these old forts remain an historical monument to those days in the seventeenth and early eighteenth centuries, when the great French engineer Vauban revolutionized defensive fortifications.

That Antwerp was so fortified is not surprising, for it was here in Flanders and Northern France where Vauban developed his system. These forts, well suited to the weapons of their day with their exact geometrical outline, offered little resistance against modern methods of assault despite efforts to modernize them and equip them with increased fire power and high angle guns.

The Naval Commander and the two demolition parties arrived safely on the north bank of the river and here they remained for five days. The Naval Commander was quite unable to negotiate permission for even a reconnaissance to be carried out. During this time the city and port were subject to endless air raids causing confusion and rumour about the extent of the German advance. Although both parties were virtually confined to their tugs, some were, for lack of space, allowed to sleep ashore in a bombed out building near to where the tugs were berthed.

The few Belgium civilians with whom our chaps had dealings were invariably friendly, but they had a much more realistic view of the impending disaster of invasion than the Dutch had shown. This is not surprising when one recalls that, in 1914, the Dutch had preserved their neutrality while Belgium had suffered invasion with all its attendant horrors and cruelties. She had seen her cities laid waste, churches desecrated, countryside pillaged and the population tortured during the long weary years of the First World War, and now, weakened with internal dissension, Belgium was facing the same grim ordeal again. Her leaders had broken away from what they thought to be entanglements with former Allies, and had emphasized their neutrality, in the vain hope of avoiding exactly what was now taking place again. The defensive role played by her army, while brave enough, was insufficiently prepared. Such help as her former Allies could give in those critical days was too late and almost entirely ineffective. One after another of her cities fell to the mechanized might of a highly organized and premeditated attack.

The German blitzkrieg tactics of puncturing the enemy with a deep and concentrated thrust or spearhead *(scherpunkt)* and then the widening of the gap *(aufrollen)* into a dangerous bulge and finally a corridor, made invasion an easy task against the unprepared Belgians. They fought stubbornly in places and held ground long enough to delay the advance here and there, but the reports which came through all told the same ominous story -- Belgium was being overrun.

It was not long before the tide reached Antwerp. Constant air attack, with all its confusion and suffering, wrought havoc upon the morale of the fleeing civilians, hordes of refugees and withdrawing Belgium troops. The invasion had acquired a momentum and weight, which only equal weight and an organized defence could halt.

The Belgians were conscious of the fact that they were even less well situated than they had been in 1914 and that their national policy towards Germany had let them down; but now it was too late. After a couple of days of air raids, with all manner of alarms and rumours, it became fairly obvious that the end was not far off. Large numbers of civilians had left the city, all ordinary life had come to a standstill and the heavy gunfire from the advancing Germans was already raining down on the suburbs. Shopkeepers had either sold out of food or their stocks had been looted. During this time the more adventurous helped themselves to any cars that were left in the town and set out towards France.

After several false starts through orders being countermanded by the Belgians, the sappers were at last reluctantly given permission for the demolition to be carried out. Some thousands of tons of fuel and lubricating oil were run out on the flat ground around the plants and subsequently into the river. While this operation was at its height, oil was flowing several feet deep and swept all before it on its way to the river. Some thousands of steel drums were also emptied before the task was completed. By this time the Germans were already occupying part of the town. However, the sappers then joined up with the Navy in their secondary role of destroying the port facilities. This they did to the best of their ability given the time available and the resources at their disposal.

Four French army lorries had been held, also under guard, on the west bank at a little place called Burght. Just as the Royal Engineer party were making their final withdrawal to that side, the naval contingent from Antwerp turned up. In spite of the Huns and the general racket from an air raid in progress at the time, this meeting raised a cheer that must have been heard in Brussels.

In a short space of time, the whole lot packed themselves into those four lorries, all too tired to stand or even sit. They just slumped onto the floor, squeezed together like sardines and set off towards the coast. They planned to go through Ghent and Bruges to Ostend where they might find a vessel. Failing that, they thought they could work their way down the coast towards one of the French channel ports. As it was getting dark when they left and the French drivers were not sure of the way, it was doubtful if they would succeed. To get an idea of the journey, one must picture all roads, large and small, packed with escaping civilians trudging along on foot, or cycling, with others riding in vehicles of every description. These poor, desperate and hungry folk were moving towards France, or the coast, to escape the vengeance of the enemy. Many had been on the move for several days, and as food could not be bought from the empty or looted shops, their plight was pitiful. Periodically, planes would dive low over the columns and machine-gun them at crossroads, jamming the route with dead and dying. After 9 p.m. the refugees were forbidden to remain on the roads and were compelled to take to the neighbouring fields until daylight. During the night the roads were equally packed, but with troop movements; infantry, horse-drawn wagons and guns, mechanized units and ambulance convoys, all jostled in that hectic withdrawal. The refugees at the side of the roads would cry out to the passing troops to throw them food. At intervals, a plane would fly over and drop a flare to be followed a few seconds later by bombers seeking out troop concentrations. They did not have to look far, more or less any stretch of road gave them a tempting target.

Their four trucks rumbled on through the night making slow progress. They were stopped frequently for identity checks. This gave rise to painful negotiations at times, as the French drivers wisely refused to be implicated in the madness of the passengers and disclaimed all knowledge of the party or their destination. The suspicions of the police were, under the circumstances, justifiable, since to be quite fair, it must be admitted that the sleeping men inside the wagons did not respond to enquiries when roughly roused to semi-consciousness. When asked 'Where are you going?' they usually shouted something like 'Blighty'. This happened repeatedly as they struggled on through the night. At times the leading driver would stop and ask the way; then suspicions would be aroused and the same wretched business would start all over again. At other times a German air-attack would bring the column to an abrupt halt.

It remained at a standstill until the maimed men or stricken vehicles were dragged off the road and then they would go on again until the next stop. Inside the lorry the exhausted men slept as if drugged, packed on the floor, man to man; as one of the men said, 'Like ruddy carcasses from Smithfield'. Just before daybreak they arrived at Ostend only to find the port abandoned and not a ship in sight. They had no alternative but to carry on down the coast to Dunkirk before they could hope to get a passage to England. The expedition eventually managed to board a train ferry at Dunkirk just before the vessel put to sea. On board they were given food, and after a wash, began to find their feet again. Their tongues began to wag, the sailors and sappers swapping the experiences of the last few days on their respective jobs. All recalled how, in the first few days a sapper had kept them supplied with pigeons, when food was difficult to obtain. He climbed on to a roof overlooking a tower where the birds roosted and with the skilful use of his catapult and much patience kept the pot full. By common consent, this was an outstanding performance and would have been even better but for the air raids which scared off the pigeons.

They arrived in Dover the same afternoon and made their way back to the unit at Gravesend. The moment they had 'fallen out' on the parade ground, they asked 'are the Dutch crowd back? We saw their destroyers bombed just before we split up!'

But they had all come back, so it was a happy day in barracks.

Chapter Five

# THE SEINE

In the early days of May 1940 the position in France was not too encouraging for the Allies and the possibility of the Germans over-running the channel ports was a serious consideration. What has now become known as the Maginot complex was not working out too well against a flanking attack through the Low Countries, and the new form of blitzkrieg as practised by the Panzer divisions of the German Army. In the light of events, it was not surprising that we were ordered to carry out a reconnaissance in great haste of the many large petrol refineries and oil installations mainly on the north bank of the River Seine between Le Havre and Rouen; easily the largest refineries and oil stocks in Europe.

In the early evening of 23 May Peter Keeble, who commanded the Amsterdam operation, was sent to Portsmouth where he boarded a destroyer that took him to Cherbourg. From there he was to motor to Rouen armed with the necessary credentials and all available information and work his way westwards from Rouen to Le Havre, at which point fresh instructions would be issued. Just before going to bed, I confirmed with the naval authorities at Portsmouth that he had joined the ship and sailed, expecting that the matter would rest there for a time at least. But I was wrong, for events over on the other side of the channel were moving quickly. The size and speed with which this operation had to be set up indicates how badly the war was going. In the original plan for XD operations it had never been envisaged that they would take place so far south.

About 11.30 p.m. on the same night, I was called from my bed by the adjutant to receive secret instructions which had just come in by dispatch rider from the Director of Military Operations. In view of the situation it did not cause much surprise when our depot was roused from its sleep and transport lorries were loaded with the type of stores which are normally kept in the magazine. A parade of sections was held in the utter blackness, details checked up, and in the small hours of the morning the convoy drew out of the barrack yard and headed successively for Chatham, Canterbury and Dover. Passing through Chatham one saw a few riotous folk still making merry in the streets, which called forth words of encouragement and advice from the troops. This banter reached its zenith when we passed a policeman urging a solitary sailor to go home; naturally all were on the side of Jolly Jack. Apart from these incidents it was a quiet, sleepy countryside through which we rumbled on one of those marvellous nights of early summer, pulling in at Dover at 6 a.m. and going straight to the harbour. The, by now familiar, stores were rapidly unloaded on to the quay and were then stowed aboard a tender, and the vehicles were sent back to the depot at Gravesend. Two destroyers were waiting out in the harbour; one for a naval demolition party and one for us. It was not long before we steamed out to our destroyer, transferred onto her decks and made all snug. This time it was not necessary to advise the men what a destroyer deck can be like when at speed in choppy weather. They now knew.

To the ordinary landsman, a voyage in these little ships under active service conditions is one to remember; the way they plough through at high speed throbbing from stem to stern is thrilling. The vibration up on the bridge when first experienced is quite uncanny. If anything of a sea is running the vessel shudders from each bump, as she plunges through succeeding waves and is swept from end to end with green sea, this swirls along the limited deck space with violence and carries anything loose overboard. The wind keeps up a steady whine in the rigging and at times it seems to take one's breath away. Now add the effect of an enemy plane raking one with machine-gun fire, bombs 'plomping' uncomfortably near and throwing up tons of water, plus the ships own ack-ack crew giving back all they can at the same time, and you have the picture. It may seem nothing to those grand fellows who

41

man the destroyers, but to a soldier it is an experience not easily forgotten. During our passages in these hard worked little vessels, the sapper parties began to make friends. When they boarded a vessel in which they had travelled before, the ship's company would greet them as old friends with some such remark as 'you here again – what is it in aid of this time?' One only hopes that the marvellous work and exploits of these hard worked destroyers during the difficult days of 1940 will be told some day. It should be an inspiration to all Englishmen.

It transpired that our ship had just come off an evacuation job during the night; hence her decks were littered with arms, equipment, old clips of rifle ammunition and so forth. The wardroom had been used as a dressing station and for surgery, so we officers munched our breakfast sandwiches amongst traces of the surgeon's busy night's work. The all pervading smell of medicaments and various odds and ends strewn about helped to remind one of the grim reality but, having been in the keen early morning air, we were hungry so the surroundings did not matter. With the usual kind hospitality of the Navy we were all given a steaming hot mug of tea to wash down our sandwiches.

The two ships awaited the signal to sail until just after 9 a.m. when we steamed out of the harbour, took station line ahead and set a south-westerly course for Le Havre. The sea was smoother than we had ever seen it before which, coupled with the brilliant sun and almost cloudless sky, gave the party a chance to sit up and take notice. Only two minor incidents occurred during the crossing, one a floating mine and later, out in mid-channel, a speck appeared in the sky. With the clear visibility obtaining at the time, all eyes turned to the aircraft. However she turned out to be one of ours and after coming down and circling round us apparently satisfied herself that we were British and flew off down the Channel. So it was that, unlike some former experiences, we ran into the harbour at Le Havre without hindrance soon after 3 p.m. and berthed along side the quay. Immediately our party manhandled their gear ashore onto the adjacent covered wharf and the destroyer put to sea again. Our little force of twelve officers and 120 other ranks, together with warlike stores, was again on foreign soil thanks to the Royal Navy. I went up to the

British HQ in the town, while the party moved off to that most cheerless of all human institutions – the transit camp. Unlike in Holland and Belgium the Seine lay on the lines of communication of the British Expeditionary Force.

At Area HQ a General Intelligence Report was obtained together with the name and location of the General Officer Commanding at Rouen, to whom I was referred for more detailed information and authority. This resulted in my setting off in a staff car, together with our adjutant, Captain Joe Hawes, to Rouen about sixty miles inland. Progress was difficult as the French, by this time alarmed by the German advance, were improvising every possible form of roadblock at vulnerable points along the fine stretch of road connecting the two cities. Looking back on those farm wagons drawn across the road, derelict cars and similar junk, manned solely by riflemen, French sailors and, at places, the *Gardes Républicaines*, as their only answer to Hitler's mechanized divisions, one could not help feeling the futility of it all. All the same, we had to get out of the car about twenty times and, in execrable French, argue our way through; this resulted in our arriving in Rouen at about midnight. It did not take long to find the Railway Transport Officer, always a safe bet in a strange place, and a telephone conversation fixed an appointment with the General Officer Commanding at British HQ for 8 a.m. the following morning. The adjutant and I parked the car up a side street, immobilized it and, while wandering through the deserted and blacked out streets, found our way to the premier hotel of the place. This was our last link with a civilized mode of life for some time to come.

We met the Commander at British HQ the following morning but the information that was needed was elsewhere; similarly the authority for our demolitions was vested in the general of the local French District HQ, who was responsible for the area we had in view. The General Officer Commanding kindly fixed up an appointment with the French general and took us over to his HQ later in the morning. It was quartered, as in peacetime, in an imposing building in the centre of the town, with an atmosphere of importance. Staff officers in impeccable uniforms, the majority with rows of medal ribbons, which for colour would have competed with an herbaceous border, moved about the corridors from room to room. After the requisite introductions, the adjutant and I were shown into the presence of *Mon General*. He was an elderly man with fine features, penetrating eyes and, like his various aides, immaculately dapper in appearance. For one moment my gaze lighted on the adjutant and then on my own uniform and I realized that battle dress was not designed to compete with these sort of surroundings. The general listened to our story, asked many questions about our mission, obviously dismissed the idea that the Germans could ever get to Rouen, and said so with emphasis and obvious amusement. 'How could it be otherwise, with the French armies between the enemy and this area?' he asked. Another polite conversation regarding the location of the installations and the suggestion that we could, at least, guard the plants from sabotage and he eventually agreed to our moving into the plants, providing we came directly under his command which he, in turn, would delegate to his technical officer responsible for the supply of *essence*!

Once outside the Headquarters, I thanked the British Commander for his kind offices in giving me the introduction that resulted in a satisfactory solution and said goodbye to him. Thus our party came under command of the French Army HQ and the adjutant and I found ourselves accompanying the technical officer, a captain of artillery, to his office in another part of the town.

Then the fun began. The French officer spoke about as much English as I spoke French and, if not hostile, was at least suspicious of both us and our mission. Furthermore, all arrangements were in his hands to protect *les usines* (the works). Moreover his arrangements were complete down to the last detail, so what more could these British soldiers do? And so on. After hours of re-iteration – to the English ear it seems to take the French so long to say so little – and by using all the diplomacy we could muster, we eventually got him to agree that our party could place a few troops at each installation, subject to further negotiation with the directors at each place! We subsequently found these to be twenty-nine in number. The French officer insisted on conducting these deliberations at which we could be present, so altogether it looked like a job for life. All this, with the Germans battering their way through the Allied Armies, made us feel rather dejected.

The same afternoon I drove back to Le Havre with some of the requisite information in my possession and a general idea of the geographical distribution of the tasks ahead. It will be remembered that Keeble had sailed from England via Cherbourg, a few hours ahead of the main party on the same errand, but, as he was not aware of the urgency when he left, I was doubtful as to when he would arrive back at Le Havre. Much detailed information was needed quickly if a successful plan was to be made. This could only be done locally at each place, hence my anxiety to get the parties out to the appropriate areas, based upon the information we had obtained so far. To our great joy Peter Keeble was found when we arrived back at the port. He had had the shock of his life when he reported to HQ and was told we were already here and in the transit camp! Naturally he imagined that the unit was still at our base at home waiting for his report. By a lucky chance his data very largely completed the gaps in the information already available, uncannily so in fact, with the result that during the same afternoon I sent about half the party off to Rouen in trucks that they had acquired. Military Operations at the War Office had sent a request ahead asking all units to give every assistance to our unit as it would be arriving in France without transport. As a result we managed to beg, borrow or steal one 15cwt truck for each section.

From a plan of Rouen we had bought in the town that morning, a rendezvous was arranged in the centre of the town, at the approach to a bridge over the river. This seemed fairly straight-forward. It was my intention to leave Le Havre later as, apart from the fact that my car was a good deal faster than the trucks, I had a number of administrative details to be settled before I could get away. I left during the late evening with the adjutant and, taking advantage of the remaining daylight, put in some good bursts of speed between the road blocks. With the approach of dusk, however, a shot from one of the many posts caused us to approach them with more caution.

Earlier in the day some German motorized patrols had allegedly broken through and approached to a point about twenty miles from Rouen, shooting up everything, in the now familiar technique of the German thrusts. The people of the surrounding countryside took fright, resulting in the town being congested with refugees struggling westwards. Convoys of ambulances were removing wounded from the railway station adding to the already chaotic traffic situation. Towards midnight a thunderstorm, with a deluge of rain, brought everything to a standstill, but eventually we arrived at the agreed rendezvous. This was in a small open space facing the road approach to the bridge over the Seine; one of two large masonry bridges which connect the north and south portions of the town.

I sat in the car and viewed the feverish preparation for demolition proceeding on the bridge. Gangs of men were cutting out about half a dozen chambers with the aid of compressors, both in the haunches and arches of the several large spans. Within a few minutes of my arrival, up came a French tank and planted itself near the car so that it commanded the approaches. This was hastily followed by wiring and sandbagging to convert the site into a permanently defended locality.

Meanwhile the adjutant had gone to explore the approaches to the other bridge as there were no signs of the convoy. Just then a squad of French infantry came upon the scene and installed themselves as defenders of the strong point. They took one look at me and my batman driver, Corporal Holland, and decided forthwith that we were fifth columnists waiting to aid the Germans over the river. I was arrested and conducted to a police post in a depressing little street nearby. The head man was out, so they said, and so I could not be examined yet. This looked like becoming a stalemate but eventually I managed to get away and back to the car with an escort who was instructed to accompany the adjutant and myself out of the town. On arrival at the car the batman driver reported that when the adjutant had returned, having seen nothing of the party, he too had been 'taken off'. At this point I succeeded in persuading the escort and the troops manning the post that if they were really anxious to get rid of us they must assist in returning the other missing British Officer. As they were in a hurry to get rid of the doubtful strangers, quite apart from who or what we were, this worked wonders and it was not long before Hawes was returned but without his revolver. By this time it was dawn and by a stroke of good luck, the trucks came lumbering over the bridge and we all moved off together to a destination just outside the town

We all arrived at a British petrol filling station, which I had decided to make our temporary headquarters, at about five a.m. and having established our credentials we were admitted, fed and bedded down in some stables at the rear of the Royal Army Service Corps Petrol Filling Depot. The OC was a cheery old Scot who, in addition to his flair for highland hospitality, knew of all the local plants and petrol installations. This proved invaluable in completing the information upon which plans were eventually based. The following day I conferred with the French liaison officer and visited a large number of plants in the vicinity. By the afternoon small sections of sappers were, by arrangements with the civilian management, posted in each installation. The experiences of these small detachments and their life for the next couple of weeks in their widely varying surroundings, cut off from all English speaking contacts except for the daily visit of their officer and an occasional dispatch rider, would make amusing reading. One lad occupied his off duty time by proposing to the daughter of the local *estaminet*, and could be seen any evening serving behind the bar, or entertaining the local patrons with song and dance in the true Lambeth manner.

When all preliminary work at the Rouen end of the Seine basin was complete, I returned to Le Havre to carry out the same work at the seaward end of the river. I found the other officers in the party had done much useful preliminary work, but it transpired that Le Havre, and some miles inland, was under the command of an admiral, and was in no way connected with the French Army HQ. This meant that all preliminary groundwork, starting from the top and working downwards, had to be done again. I found the admiral to be a pleasant little man, who spoke English quite well and was not as sceptical of our mission as the general. At one of the many interviews, he asked my opinion as to the best dispositions for barrage balloons of which, it should be noted, they had but six. Having discussed the matter at length the admiral terminated the discussion by saying 'If I put ballon up – the Boche, he come over and shoot him down – if I no put ballon up – what use ballon?' However he was most helpful and in a few days the troops were spread along the river towards Rouen in small sections so that all industrial plants were covered. At this point I moved my headquarters to a larger installation, just south of Rouen. This was conveniently situated for road and telephone communication with the twenty-nine objectives which our unit was to guard for the time being, and to destroy in the event of the close approach of the enemy in force.

The Seine basin from Le Havre to Rouen was divided up into six areas. The distribution of officers and their men was as follows:

| | | |
|---|---|---|
| Area No. 1 | Le Havre | Second Lieutenant D. Terry |
| Area No. 2 | Gonfreville | Second Lieutenant R. Meyler |
| Area No. 3 | Port Jerome | Captain P. Keeble |
| Area No. 4 | Mailleraye | Captain T. Goodwin |
| Area No. 5 | Rouen | Second Lieutenant P. Baker |
| Area No. 6 | Petit Couronne | Second Lieutenant Whitehead |

By far the largest installations were at Port Jerome and Mailleraye as they also included the only two oil refineries. All the other sites were purely tank farms.

The new headquarters, which overlooked a refinery, were in a large villa on a hill and had previously been occupied by its director. The place showed signs of hurried evacuation; pictures remained on the walls, some furniture had been left and the cupboards contained all the odds and ends of ordinary life. Three officers and about a dozen other ranks, mainly dispatch riders, installed themselves together with half a dozen of the *Gardes Républicaines*. The latter ostensibly to augment the guard, but actually to watch the movements of the sappers and to report each day to one of their officers, who invariably dropped in and exchanged backchat on the flesh and the Devil. This Frenchman had served in their colonial army and had a fine repertoire of yarns which served as a stimulus to conversation; however very little happened which escaped his attention. The explosives were stored in the basement of the house to which the sappers would retire during air raids. This seemed fair enough for, being below ground, nothing but a direct hit was likely to harm them, and in that case the stocks of explosives would not matter anyhow.

During the next two weeks all arrangements throughout the sixty mile belt were completed and day and night a dispatch rider shuttle service was run between all detachments and head-quarters, as by this time, it was unsafe in the interests of secrecy, to use the telephone. Each day one of the officers in Rouen would collect intelligence reports from British sources and I obtained similar information from the French Army via the liaison officer, who was evidently charged with controlling the party's actions. The comparison of these two reports, relating to the same incidents, invariably provided an interesting study of what can be done by emphasis. As any woman will tell you, it is not what you say, but the way you say it! It must be appreciated that the area was flooded with fifth columnists, spies and other enemy agents. Parachutists were captured and shot, and rumour was rife sedulously fostered no doubt by the Boche. Hence it was not really surprising that everyone was suspicious of the rest of humanity.

As far as the British sappers were concerned this atmosphere of distrust eventually culminated in my being sent for by the local French District HQ and presented with an agreement which I was ordered to sign. The only alternative was evacuation of the party which would have set at zero all efforts up to date and, in the light of subsequent experience, would undoubtedly have resulted in the plants and stocks of fuel falling into enemy hands. The document was written on four pages of foolscap in both French and English; the principal features of the document were as follows:

_Duties_ to guard all plants in the Seine basin Le Havre-Rouen, severally mentioned, against the enemies of France. That the British should stay on their stations until the last.

That they should be under French command and act only upon the French GHQ (both Army and Navy) orders as transmitted through the liaison officer.

That absolute secrecy be maintained.

That the French would provide food.

*Systems of intercommunications.*
*That if any independent action were taken on our own initiative by any member of the British party, they would be regarded as saboteurs and dealt with according to French military custom.*

A space was provided for the signatures of both parties. The situation brooked no delay and as the sappers had by now got so near their objectives, I signed on the dotted line. As I left the building my only misgiving was that when the end came, would they procrastinate? I consoled myself with the thought that in any case I would have the liaison officer with me at the end and it was hardly likely that he would quarrel over procedure in the face of the enemy.

As we were under command of the French Army they had already provided us with rations which were not of a very high order and also the obligatory issue of red wine each day. The latter came in considerable quantities but sadly was very rough and tasted like vinegar.

During the waiting time all ranks perfected their local knowledge of the objectives and the surrounding country. The enemy was getting nearer all the time and air raids, unopposed except by a few widely spaced batteries of ack-ack guns of varying calibre, became fairly regular. Towards the end of this time countless refugees streamed along the roads leading west and south; surely a more pathetic sight never existed. There were men, women, children, at times with their livestock and even domestic animals. Young and old, rich and poor, these wretched people surged along those straight roads in a never ending stream, away from *la guerre* toward what they hoped would be a happier land.

What disillusionment was in store for those weary travellers. One would see the large four wheeled farm carts of the country packed with their belongings; the family, ranging from grandparents to little children and babies perched high on top, dogs trotting along underneath. Pots and pans suspended below carts rattled a dirge with every forward movement. In front the team of struggling horses, usually steaming from their heavy pull, were urged along by the farmer tugging at their heads, the remaining male members of the family either whipping up the horses or

50

pushing behind the wagon according to their strength. Next in procession would come a large, showy saloon car packed with the more important or valued possessions of the owners, a mattress tied on the top of the vehicle and well dressed folk inside. The driver, as is customary in France, operating his hooter most of the time in his impatience to get on. One would also see young men trudging along pushing bicycles loaded high with bundles of gargantuan proportions; how they ever got their load poised was a mystery. To swell this sorrowful trail were less fortunate members of society just plodding along carrying bags, suitcases or even small bundles; their sole possessions. Unlike their usual custom, there was little conversation among these people. All were sad and weary, for some of the older ones this was the second time they had left their homes to escape the savagery of the Hun. Some had come from as far off as Belgium to join in this great trek to safety. When the cars broke down or ran out of fuel, they were abandoned by the roadside or in some field; similarly those walking when too weary, just dropped down by the roadside to forget their misery in sleep. Periodically the German planes came over, flying low above those long straight roads. They either fired their machine guns while ammunition lasted or spread havoc and confusion with an occasional bomb. The injured dragged themselves aside, the dead were laid aside with the broken vehicles and the procession of human suffering moved on once again. I find it difficult to eradicate from my memory the look on the faces of those unhappy people.

During the last few day, as things grew worse, this civilian migration to the south and west was at first diluted with remnants from the French army and then gradually the roads became thronged with marching troops and the civilian element grew scarcer. At times when they halted, we would ask them where they were going, to which the same reply always came 'à Toulouse'! The whole outlook of the French seemed to be one of mere physical contact without regard to the factors of time and space; hence the German thrusts were never effectively met by any planned counterattack. It seemed as if the entire French army was going towards the Pyrenees to regroup. They looked happy enough and apparently glad to be out of the struggle. A strange feature of this progressive movement was that no wounded were noticeable and must have been left behind or taken by another route. Sometimes long convoys of vehicles replaced troops in the never ending stream and lastly came the guns, battery after battery; we knew then that the end was near.

Every day, either the adjutant, Joe Hawes, or I went round the circuit calling at the principal posts dealing with the administrative problems that cropped up during the attachment to the French army. Early in June I arrived in Le Havre on such a journey to find that one of the plants had been hit during an enemy air raid early the same morning. A fair amount of damage had been done near the docks and, at the oil installation in question, two large tanks of petrol had been destroyed. One had been blown bodily about fifty yards away and the other flattened; both were utterly wrecked. Fortunately most of the blazing spirit had run into an empty dock. Four sappers together with the night watchman fought the flames and saved the fire from spreading to the rest of the plant so justifying their official status as guards. The room normally used as their barrack room, which they left when the alert sounded, was completely wrecked. In another part of the harbour two benzine tanks blazed steadily for some hours. This was the first real raid of any severity that Le Havre had experienced and it produced a very salutary effect upon the population in the matter of taking alerts more seriously. While in the town I was told that the admiral wished to see me. He was very friendly and expressed himself as satisfied with what was being done in his area. In discussing the war he said little but, in emphasizing the necessity for constant vigilance, gave me the impression that he was not so certain about the trend of events as were the French Army and the liaison officer. Looking back upon those highly placed elderly French officers commanding areas and towns in depth behind the front, one is forced to the conclusion that they had regarded their posts as administrative sinecures. They never really expected to be faced with German armoured fighting vehicles or, for that matter, streams of suffering refugees passing through their towns. One can only think that their confidence in their defences was based upon the mistaken belief that they would never be put to the stern test of war.

At one of the bigger *usines* in a country district under our protection, a large workers' canteen and living accommodation was temporarily used as a hostel for young female refugees from northern France and Belgium. As our party was in occupation prior to this influx and doing the cooking, our detachment took on the entirely new role of organizer, comforter and general welfare adviser upon those matters which young women seek advice and guidance.

Another strange episode was an order from French HQ that we were to scour the Forêt Londe for paratroops, said to have landed early one morning. I eventually found myself in command of a small mixed command of French and English troops combing the forest; as this was about fifteen miles long and three or four miles wide, it was a fair task. The total bag was a grounded RAF fighter and one Belgian spy; a very beautiful blonde complete with caravan. I interviewed the lady, who gave me coffee and after a few minutes of French broke into English. She told an interesting story of escaping from the wicked Germans and coming with her caravan to these peaceful surroundings near the crossroads in the heart of the forest. The French liaison officer when he came upon the scene took a different view of the lady's dilemma, with the net result that she left the sylvan glades the same day *sans* caravan. The incident, however, taught us the geography of the forest, with its inter-secting roads. This information was to prove our salvation later on, although we did not appreciate it at the time.

A broadcast at that time by Ferdonnet, the French Lord Haw Haw stated that the Germans would capture the oil plants on the Seine in spite of the large British forces defending them. By the fifth of June things were getting bad; enemy planes were over the whole length of the Seine at frequent intervals and the intelligence reports from British HQ gave the situation as grave, in the face of persistent enemy attacks. The admiral at Le Havre, where many large fires were burning, gave orders for the evacuation of all but key personnel. Partial evacuation of Rouen was carried out and an ad hoc British division just outside the city was taking heavy punishment. All industrial plants were closing and their staff being sent away from the area. The last train from the city passed our HQ not only packed to a point of suffocation, but with people actually sitting outside on the roof.

At ten o'clock the British intelligence report told of enemy columns, tanks and armoured infantry all moving southwards through the gaps in the defences, of sections of the railway being bombed and stations on fire. The previous day the French had been heavily attacked from Neufchatel to Forges and the enemy was over the River Brest. Later we heard that orders had been given to Brigade Commanders to blow bridges at their discretion. At the same time our liaison officer came to our HQ with the intelligence summaries which still gave the situation as favourable, adding a rider to the effect that they expected a further engagement within two days which they confidently felt would be in their favour – it was difficult not to feel sorry for them.

An additional worry cropped up at this stage. It was the discovery in one of the plants of 10, 000 gallons of tetraethyl lead in drums, both dangerous and poisonous stuff to have on our hands in an emergency, but too important to neglect and a commodity which required special care.

The following day the sound of heavy gunfire came with the first streaks of dawn; later this was supplemented by fairly general but scattered bombing throughout the whole course of the Seine. All our dispatch riders brought in similar reports. In the afternoon the town major called at our HQ to say goodbye and to warn us about being hoodwinked by a German who was said to be in a British Staff car and was dressed as a sapper major. This bogus major turned up in Rouen the same morning, appropriately dressed and walked up to a subaltern, who had just stepped out of his car onto the pavement. The young man was very foolishly alone and unarmed, the 'major' engaged him in polite conversation and told him not to be alarmed at what he was about to witness, stepped back into the car and drove off! It is a matter of conjecture as to what the young man's feelings were when he reported the incident to his CO and what happened to him. Although I felt satisfied that no stranger would get entry to our projects I immediately spread the story to all concerned with the obvious injunctions. As the town major left and was saying

1. Brigadier C.C.H. Brazier in 1945.

2. The Unit at camp in the early 1930s.

3. Officers in camp in 1937. *Back Row: L to R:* Lieutenant Hannam, Lieutenant Cox, Lieutenant Goodwin, Lieutenant Rear, Lieutenant Buxton, Lieutenant Dent, Lieutenant Keeble, Lieutenant Wilmot.
*Front Row: L to R:* Captain Hawes, Captain West, Captain Ewbank, Major Brazier, Captain Curtis, Captain Dawson.

4. The Coronation Parade at the Clock Tower in Gravesend in 1937.

5. Kent Fortress Royal Engineers leaving the parade ground at Sheerness in 1938, headed by their own band.

6. Route march wearing respirators; part of the toughening up process!

7. Construction of trenches. In those days great emphasis was placed on beating sandbags really square, like bricks.

8. The winners of the Lord Wakefield Trophy in 1938. A real triumph for a small unit as it was shot for by all units in the Territorial Army which, at that time, consisted of no less than ten divisions. Back row, L to R: Lance Corporal Gillet, Sergeant Halliday, Lance Sergeant Smart, Sapper

9. Captain Peter Keeble.

10. Captain Tommy Goodwin.

11. Landing at Ijmuiden. *Drawing by Lance Corporal Hill.*

12. A burning oil wharf in Amsterdam. *Drawing by Lance Corporal Hill.*

13. Lance Corporal Vic
    Hugget and Sapper
    Wally Page in
    Amsterdam.  Having
    no cameras Hugget
    removed one from a
    civilian on the
    grounds that he was
    on a highly secret
    operation - hence
    this photograph and
    the following one,
    which are the only
    two to survive.

14. Burning oil tanks in Amsterdam.

15. Sappers unloading stores at the Hook of Holland from HMS *Wild Swan*. This picture apppeared in a national newspaper the following day. It must have been taken by one of the ship's company as there were no official photographers there. Much to the sappers' chagrin it was headed 'British Marines land stores in Holland'.

16. Rouen oil plants ablaze. *Drawing by Lance Corporal Hill.*

17. *Courtesy of Imperial War Museum. Neg. C1804.*

18. *Courtesy of Imperial War Museum. Neg. C1802.*

Chance photographs taken by a Coastal Command aircraft showing burning oil tanks at St Malo.

18th September, 1940.

To:-

   British Consuls, Senior Naval, Military
   and Air Commanders.

   ------------------------

         This is to certify that Major R.Keeble,R.E.
is on special duty under War Office direction.

         Please give him all assistance in your
power including transport by sea, land or air.

                                    C. JW Simpson Maja G.S.
ʃn. Director of Military Operations & Plans.

19. Major Keeble's 'magic letter'.

20. Destruction and withdrawal from Spitzbergen.

*Courtesy of Imperial War Museum. Neg. H13592.*

21. *Courtesy of Imperial War Museum. Neg. H13604.*

Destruction and withdrawal from Spitzbergen.

22. *Courtesy of Imperial War Museum. Neg. H13600.*

23. Ice floes.                                    *Drawing by Lance Corporal Hill.*

24. The Norwegian settlement of Longyearby.       *Drawing by Lance Corporal Hill.*

25. Demolition was carried out at Ny Alesund, Longyearby, Sveagruva, Pyramiden, Grumantby and Barentsburg.                    *Drawing by Lance Corporal Hill.*

26. Coal stocks on fire.                    *Drawing by Lance Corporal Hill.*

# EIGHT ROYAL ENGINEERS HONOURED

## Decorations For Local Officers And N.C.O's.

## "DISTINGUISHED SERVICE IN THE FIELD"

Capt. T. F. Goodwin

Capt. R. Keeble

Corp. J. Mitten

Staff-Sergt. A. H. Smart

Sergt. J. Hearnden

Lieut.-Col. C. C. H. Brazier

Capt. B. Buxton

Sergt. A. R. Blake

Our readers will be proud to learn that eight local Royal Engineers have been awarded decorations for gallantry on active service.

This is the longest list of local military awards ever issued.

Before the outbreak of war these officers and non - commissioned officers were members of a Kent Territorial Army unit associated with the local cement industry.

Published on Saturday morning, the official announcement stated:

"The King has approved of the following appointment and awards in recognition of distinguished services in the field":—

### O.B.E. (MILITARY DIVISION).

Major (Bt. Lieut.-Col.) acting Lieut.-Col. C. C. H. BRAZIER, M.B.E., J.P., M.I.Mech.E., A.M.I.E.E.

### DISTINGUISHED SERVICE ORDER.

Captain R. KEEBLE.

Captain T. F. GOODWIN.

Captain B. BUXTON, B.Sc. (Eng.), A.M.I.Mech.E.

### DISTINGUISHED CONDUCT MEDAL.

Corpl. J. T. HEARNDEN.

### MILITARY MEDAL.

Staff-Sergt. A. H. SMART.

Sergt. A. R. BLAKE.

Corpl. J. MITTEN.

Lt.-Col. Brazier is one of the best known personalities in this district. He was manager of Bevan's Cement Works, and a former Chairman of Northfleet Urban District Council. His residence is "Proctors," Southfleet. He has had a distinguished career in the Royal Engineers. During the last war he served in Mesopotamia and India and was mentioned in despatches.

For some years he commanded the Kent (Fortress) R.E., was given Brevet promotion and awarded the M.B.E. before the war, and later appointed C.R.E. to the Kent Corps Troops Engineers. He served with the B.E.F. in France, and is a military member of the Kent T.A. Association. Well-known in rifle shooting circles, he was County champion in 1930. He is a member of the Institution of Mechanical Engineers, an associate member of the Institution of Electrical Engineers, and Assistant Commissioner for No. 1 Area (Kent) St. John Ambulance Brigade.

Captain (now Major) R. Keeble resided in Gravesend for some years, and was a well-known Company Commander in a local Territorial unit for several years. He passed through the staff college, and served with the B.E.F. in Holland and France. Has shot for the county and the Territorial Army and was a member of the team which won the Lord Wakefield Cup, open to Great Britain.

Captain T. F. Goodwin, who lived in Gravesend, served in the local Sappers for some years. He was county champion rifle shot in 1934, and served with the B.E.F. in Holland and France. He is well-known in boxing and sporting circles.

Captain B. Buxton lived in Northfleet, and also served in a local R.E. (T.A.) unit. He played Rugby for Bevan's team, and served with the B.E.F. in Holland and France.

Cpl. (now Sergt.) Hearnden's home is at 12, Lawn-road, Northfleet. An ex-Regular, he has served for eight years in the T.A. He is a well-known Rugby player and a boxer of repute. He served with the B.E.F. in Holland and France.

Staff-Sergt. Smart lives at 57, Station-street, Northfleet. He served eight years in the T.A. and is a well-known rifle shot in county shooting circles. Played cricket for the Kent (Fortress) Royal Engineers before the war. Served with the B.E.F. in France.

Sergt. A. R. Blake's home is also in Northfleet. His parents live at 169, Park-avenue. He served some years in the T.A., and a short while in the Royal Marines. Was recently married. This photograph was taken on his wedding day. Served with the B.E.F. in Holland and France.

Corpl. Mitten's home is at 71, Hampton-crescent, Gravesend. He served for some years in the T.A., for which he has shot in inter-Service matches. Is a member of the regimental band and a popular figure.

27. Honours and Awards. Cutting from the *Gravesend and Dartford Reporter*, 7 December 1940. See Appendix II for details.

28. Salver presented to Clifford Brazier on giving up command. The reverse lists the remarkable number of places in which the Unit operated during the first two years of the war.

29. Survivors at a Sixtieth Anniversary party at Gravesend in May 2000. *L to R*: Albert Ashby, Ben Dowe, Alf Blake MM and Reginald Hicks.

goodbye, he expressed the view that Rouen would be occupied before morning and told me enough to convince me that his views were well founded. By this time the writing was on the wall.

I sat down with my guide, philosopher and friend, the adjutant, and between us we drafted final orders covering the party's last job in this sector of France. Everything was in readiness and arrangements outlined for withdrawal by small groups to a rendezvous fixed in the market square of St Pierre some thirty miles to the west. Having sent these orders out in the early evening, we fed and had baths, on the grounds that it might be some time before another opportunity occurred, and went to sleep with the now commonplace thump of bombs and the crack of the ack-ack gunners' reply, as a background to receding consciousness.

Towards 9.00 p.m. an orderly woke us up with an urgent message from the French liaison officer to go down to the nearby plant at once. As we went down from the villa there was a fairly good clatter going on up in the hills on the other side of the river and an air raid seemed to be in progress over Rouen. The news was that the general had ordered all sections to stand prepared on one hour's notice. We got this over by telephone in code to some of the plants but the more distant installations had to be advised by dispatch riders working along the small roads. All night, until 2.00 a.m. the following day this state of tension remained, with everybody at their posts spread out amongst those ghostly oil tanks, now hardly discernible in the pitch black summer night. Meantime the gunfire and general racket continued. It was the same at Le Havre, but the intermediate places along the river were quiet.

After 2.00 a.m. gunfire seemed to be taking place behind us a few miles away as well as across the river. This was somewhat disturbing. I asked the French officer to either let us get on with the job or at least to urge such a course on his HQ as there seemed a fair chance of the Germans capturing the place lock, stock and barrel. The French either ignored his request or procrastinated; to give them their due they had a lot on their hands during those last few hours. At 2.30 a.m. a staff officer from the French District HQ, came dashing in with the news that the enemy had passed by

Rouen, crossed the Seine at Elbeuf about eight miles away and circled round all the nineteen installations in the horseshoe bend of the river in the Rouen district. It was not absolutely clear if they had got across all roads and we took a chance and sent our dispatch riders to all our sections with instructions to blow on the close approach of the enemy in force, unless previously ordered to do so. I also sent a message saying that I had decided in view of the very confused situation now prevailing, instead of rendezvousing as arranged, all sections should make their own way south-west to St Nazaire. The dual control from naval and military sources made things a bit tricky at this stage and one was anxious that this job should not slip through our fingers. The dawn came, then daylight, and at last at 5.00 a.m. the word came through that the French HQ had withdrawn during the night and that we were to blow up all the twenty-nine installations at 5.45 a.m., i.e. in three-quarters of an hours' time! It was also alleged that we were cut off! This was our last contact with the French HQ. Meantime the general racket increased, rifle fire and the nearby stutter of machine guns seemed to confirm this last communication quite convincingly. As security did not matter at this point, we telephoned most of the plants to order them, in clear, to carry out final demolitions, at the appointed 5.45 a.m. and we sent dispatch riders to the others, with instructions to the riders not to come back here but to throw in their lot with the last section they visited.

So, 5.45 a.m. one fine summer morning, twenty-nine refineries and oil storage plants with just over a million tons of fuel and lubricating oil were fired. The method used was the well tried one of earlier XD operations in the Low Countries; the blowing of the outlet valves with gun cotton and then, when a sufficient pool of oil had formed inside the bund, their firing. In the case of pools of only bunker oil, blankets soaked in kerosene were used.

The conflagration was probably one of the biggest of its time, extending as it did over sixty miles along the riverfront. The flames were several hundred feet high and above all a dense pall of black smoke again several hundred feet thick, drifted slowly over the surrounding country. The fires were punctuated with explosions; some were from our charges while others were simply caused by partly full tanks getting very hot, exploding and taking off into the air.

Joe Hawes and I pulled out and drove down the road, south-west, too tired to worry much, with St Pierre in mind. As our car climbed on to high ground we looked back and could trace the course of the river for many miles by the large areas of fire. The most amazing feature was the darkness and chill due to the pall of smoke cutting off the sun's rays. This was particularly notice-able over the central sectors where the very large plants were situated.

My batman, Holland, was driving and we had not been going long before we came to a crossroads and ran right into what appeared to be a scrap between a French seventy-five battery and some German vehicles. The Germans appeared to be in some force and it was either capture or evasive action; a burst of machine-gun fire was enough to promote a quick decision. As this was on the outskirts of the Forêt Londe, the scene of the spy hunt, it did not take us long to turn off the road into one of the rides cut through the trees and onto a minor road leading towards the coast. Underneath the trees were thousands of refugees in varying states of exhaustion. Progress was well nigh impossible at times as they clung round the car begging for lifts, food or water. Moreover craters in the road from recent bombing raids, necessitated detours over rough ground making progress difficult; at one place where a single railway line formed a level crossing with the road, the car had to take a detour into the forest for some distance.

At 10.00 a.m. we arrived at the rendezvous not particularly expecting to meet any of the sections. Nevertheless St Pierre was more or less on the direct route south-west for some of them so I was not too surprised when up came several of our sections who had been operating midway between Le Havre and Rouen. The latter reported that all had gone according to plan and the fires of adjacent plants could be seen as far as Le Havre. They had crossed the Seine without casualty but were exhausted after hours of standing to, ready to carry out the demolitions and suffering from hunger. Later, other groups, operating nearer the estuary, passed through telling a similar story and confirming that the Le Havre plants had been blown up, with the enemy on the outskirts of the town. We had heard from Lieutenant Don Terry, our officer in charge that his party was going to withdraw seawards in a British destroyer after helping out with the demolition of the port installations. Other sections were now also pulling out after having completed their tasks. Nearly all the plants were on the north or wrong side of the river for withdrawal. The first bridges over the Seine from Le Havre at the mouth of the river were at Rouen. However there were a number of ferries that might or might not be operational. When the situation had become critical most of the section officers had sent their 15cwt trucks over to the south bank. In the original operation order for the Seine operation the sections were warned that they might have to construct rafts in order to get back over the river after firing the oil. In the event this did not prove necessary. There were as many as a dozen men on some of these 15cwt trucks designed for six men in the back. Fortunately there was a comfortable perch for two men to sit between the bonnet and the front mudguards, which helped to relieve congestion.

By now most of the men were accounted for, which was reassuring news. Later I set out with the adjutant and Corporal Holland to make Nantes the same day. We had reason to believe that we could telephone to England from there as it was in use as a British base. I was anxious to report the conclusion of our mission and to get directions for any further tasks.

The long drive of over 200 miles was difficult and it was almost impossible to keep awake, so we each took it in turns at the wheel, while the other two immediately sank into oblivion. Travelling against time, making the best speed we could in the circumstances, we nearly piled up a dozen times when the one driving lapsed into a semi-comatose state. Towards the end, we were changing places every fifteen minutes as no one could be trusted to stay awake! It was late that night when we pulled into the British HQ at Nantes. Having spoken to Military Operations at the War Office in England by telephone and reported our arrival to the duty officer at the local HQ, we were directed to a rest camp at Savenay about twenty miles along the road to St Nazaire. This last stage was about the limit of our endurance. Fortunately it was pitch black, so that we had to crawl. It was about midnight when we entered the camp and fell in a heap on the floor of the first vacant hut. All three participants still regard this most curious journey as half dream, half reality.

## Chapter Six

# EVACUATION

Savenay was a rest camp between Nantes and St Nazaire, situated just above the small Breton town in pleasant open country. The huts were built near what appeared to have been the local racecourse and very few troops were in occupation. It was presided over by an elderly gunner subaltern who had been a ranker in the First World War and knew what the men wanted so he applied himself with some diligence to making the place comfortable. When our sections arrived, after their withdrawal from the Seine and the long trek westwards across France, Savenay seemed like a benediction on the weary travellers. Here they could eat, bathe and sleep without even an air raid. This lasted for several days. An occasional visit to the local *estaminet* enabled them to listen to wireless reports from the BBC and Radio Paris, at the same time as sampling the excellent meals and marvellous cellar. Life would have been fairly kind but for the ominous news reports.

When all the sections had got back to Savenay, apart from Don Terry's party, it transpired that the oil tanks at Honfleur across the Seine estuary from Le Havre had not been destroyed. The omission had come about because the officer in charge of the most westerly of the oil installations at Le Havre, Don Terry, had been under naval command at the port and had not appreciated that the Honfleur tank farm was part of his 'show'. Don Terry and his section, after helping to destroy the port installations had, as you will remember, already left for England on a destroyer.

Tommy Goodwin with Second Lieutenant Whitehead, Lance Sergeant Ward and about eight sappers very courageously volunteered to go back the whole way to Honfleur despite the very fluid situation as regards mechanized German patrols.

When I arrived at Savenay I found that Peter Keeble, who had done the original reconnaissance, had arrived before us and had moved out with his party on his own initiative to tackle another dump. He had been advised when he initially came over to France, not only of the details of the Seine installations but, in passing, he was told that there was an enormous BEF fuel dump in the forest of Blain down near St Nazaire. Although it had nothing to do with our tasks on the Seine, he had remembered this information.

The dump turned out to be of considerable size and area. Here at Blain was a prize indeed for the Germans. The huge dump of petrol in forty gallon drums and four gallon tins were in well separated piles as a precaution against fire accidentally spreading. These were piled up in square stacks leading far into the forest with a complete network of roadways and paths. It stored the main BEF stocks of petrol and aviation spirits for the RAF. Despite the obvious hazards in tackling this dump Keeble made the very courageous decision to carry on although he was doing it on his own initiative. This task was quite different from any of the previous ones and in any case by now they had expended all their explosives. They had no alternative but to resort to the highly dangerous practice of breaking open the drums of volatile liquid with pickaxes and bayonets; sparks were inevitable. The weather was hot and it had not rained for some days so everything was tinder dry. When they had finished holing a few of the drums in every pile, the smell of petrol vapour inside the forest was almost overpowering. In these circumstances Keeble decided to light the dump at the upwind end and allow the wind and burning tinder to do the rest of the job. The party withdrew to the upwind side of the wood and Keeble ignited the nearest drums by firing a Very Light cartridge into the petrol on the ground; the fire spread at a frightening pace down the length of the whole wood. One pile of drums had accidentally caught fire prematurely, nobody was quite sure how, and two men came out very badly burned. And at the end of the task when Keeble checked the numbers there was one man missing. Though they searched for him as best they could it was impossible to get inside the forest which was now engulfed in flames and sadly what happened to him will never be known. The two men with burns survived and happily made it back to England.

Through the last peaceful day or two that ensued we had little accurate knowledge of what was happening. Daily intelligence reports collected from British HQ at Nantes told at first of enemy pressure and withdrawals, but latterly the situation became more confused. The French radio news distribution, right up to the last, glossed over the true state of affairs and was usually rounded off by encouraging speeches and appeals to the nation by ministers. They extolled the French army and encouraged the people to stand firm. Life at Nantes seemed to be going on very much the same as in peacetime; there was little attempt at blackout and cars used headlamps at night!

Towards the end of the week I went to the local HQ and , as I went up the drive, I noticed that smoke was issuing from the chimneys and a party was burning papers at the side of the house! This looked ominous enough – I had seen the same thing before earlier in the campaign. The Commander told me that things were pretty bad and that he could not say more at the moment but he was obviously a worried man.

As I was leaving the building, I met an acquaintance who rather shocked me; firstly by telling me that he knew the purpose of our mission, which was a closely guarded secret, and secondly that he felt it was his duty to tell me that the French were about to conclude an armistice. Apparently the British had been given a brief spell to effect a withdrawal from France. He volunteered the information that French resistance had almost ceased and the Germans were marching westwards practically unopposed. This put an end to the brief peaceful existence at Savenay. Before leaving I found the name and address of an RASC officer connected with petrol supplies who had an intimate knowledge of the local installations, and immediately set out to find him. The officer was run to earth at the Donges refinery just outside St Nazaire. At first he was, quite naturally loath to talk, but after having impressed upon him the serious implications and consequent dangers of these supplies falling into enemy hands, he put me 'in the picture' and cooperated fully. Time was pressing. To cut a long story short, a party was sent out to Donges immediately upon my return and demolition was timed for 9.00 p.m. that evening. Back at Savenay the remaining sections were getting ready to move to St Nazaire at midnight for, by this time, the order for general evacuation had been made for the remainder of British Forces in that part of France. They were tramping their weary way towards the roads leading to the port.

Plans were partly upset by a telephone call from a certain irate British general who forbade any action at either place! As I was speaking I could see the familiar red glow in the sky some miles away towards Blain and the black pall above the flames drifting slowly across the forest. I diplomatically didn't mention this fact! Unfortunately I had no alternative but to send out an urgent message by dispatch rider to Donges which arrived just in time to cancel that demolition. There is no doubt that the enemy used this place, with its stocks of fuel oil, as a fuelling depot for submarines. When we heard the BBC news reports that the RAF had been over Donges we always had a pang of remorse – if only that dispatch rider had sustained a puncture or had ridden into a ditch! Our great consolation was that the BEF dump at Blain was destroyed, thanks to Peter Keeble's timely initiative.

At midnight the party moved off towards St Nazaire. The going was difficult as will be imagined, for the roads were packed with troops. Some were on foot, others in transport ranging from many kinds of army vehicles to bicycles. RAF lorries were bringing in large numbers of ground staff. Nurses, doctors and, in fact, a fairly large cross section of the Expeditionary Force found themselves, at daybreak, converging upon that coastal town which was already packed with waiting troops.

I decided to leave one section behind under Second Lieutenant Paul Baker to carry out any final demolitions that the local commander might require including Donges if there was a change of heart. However no further demolitions were authorized as it was felt that it might hinder any possible French defensive action. The local commander sent this section back on 22 June on a collier already very heavily laden with troops that had hurriedly been pressed into service to help in the evacuation. The journey was uneventful and they made Falmouth in about twenty-four hours; relieved to have arrived back safely but incredibly hungry.

The large semi-circular bay with its wide sands, esplanade and ornamental public gardens was packed with the British Army to an extent that obliterated the natural colours and rendered the whole panorama a monochrome of khaki. Back in the town too, units of every description were either halted or moving at funereal pace back to the docks. Near the docks the scene changed to blue as the RAF were concentrating at this point. Far out in the bay, it seemed two or three miles away, were anchored several large transports with grey hulls shimmering in the sunlight, reflected from the placid blue sea.

All eyes were turned to those ships and we watched several small craft plying to and fro between the docks and the ships all day long. The embarkation staff worked wonders under difficult circumstances, keeping a steady control over the waiting thousands and, in cooperation with the naval authorities, performed miracles with the very limited facilities at their disposal. The men were good-humoured if not exactly patient, but frightfully sick at having to 'leave it to Jerry' as they expressed their feelings. Towards midday a single enemy plane flew over the town and harbour and reconnoitred the surging crowds below. There was no question of taking cover as there were too many of us. The usual alert was sounded and after the intruder had flown off in an easterly direction, the 'all clear' restored the former calm. Our party, except for the redoubtable Tommy Goodwin and his team of volunteers who had not yet arrived back from Honfleur, were put off during the afternoon to the *Duchess of York* with about 5,000 others packed like herrings. Every bit of alleyway, cabin, and between-deck space was filled.

Soon after 3.00 p.m. the ship's complement was full. As we lay at anchor in the sunny bay the tired troops quickly stretched out on every available bit of space and slept. About 4 .00 p.m. we were wakened by the liner's ack-ack guns in action. It was a raid but without harm as the bombs fell wide of the mark, dropping some hundred yards or so astern. The other three waiting transports were equally fortunate. We remained at anchor in the bay for some hours before eventually leaving harbour, during which time the Hun plane came back with monotonous regularity, but always at great height.

Once under way, the voyage was uneventful. Food was scarce but in a couple of days we were landed at Liverpool.

When we arrived the Military Port Authorities had been ordered to send all the various 'cap badges' disembarking, who were from dozens of different units, straight to their regimental depots by train for sorting. At the outbreak of the war the sapper depot had been moved from Chatham to Halifax in Yorkshire. As we were more or less a complete formed body, I could not accept this. I went to the local bus depot and requisitioned sufficient buses to take us to London. The sappers were delighted as they had no wish to be herded off to the depot in Halifax. We stopped for a meal in Stafford on our way down and arrived at Charing Cross, the station for Gravesend, an hour or two after midnight. We were advised that an all night canteen was run by ladies in the crypt of St Martin-in-the-Fields in Trafalgar Square under the auspices of the Revd 'Tubby' Clayton of Toc H. When we got there at 3.00 a.m. they served us all with a wonderful traditional English breakfast. We then moved back to Charing Cross station where I left Peter Keeble in charge until I returned. I told him that I was going to Military Operations at the War Office firstly to report back and secondly to get permission to stand the unit down for seven days' leave. He was to wait with the men until I got back.

The men were naturally exhausted and like all soldiers decided to lie down and rest all over the platform. A commuter train came in shortly and the passengers all took pity on our chaps and gave them half crowns to help them buy food. I got unexpectedly held up at the War Office and as a result several commuter trains came in in quick succession. The men were repeatedly given money by the generous hearted British public as each train emptied. Their pay being only two shillings a day, this was a bonus that they were not used to. At one point the Station Master told Keeble that he must move the men away but he stood his ground saying that they had strict orders to remain where they were. I eventually got back and we returned by the next train to Gravesend and all the men went on seven days' leave much better off financially.

Goodwin and his party, despite their misgivings, had no

difficulty getting back to Honfleur where they found everything very quiet, in fact there were still a few British Base troops there. The senior British Officer was a sapper lieutenant colonel and he took Goodwin under his wing and arranged for our men to be billeted in an empty RASC petrol depot. Regular meals were provided for the men in a restaurant. The town was nearly deserted and no air raids were being carried out by the enemy air force but German soldiers were clearly visible across the estuary in Le Havre. The party were in Honfleur nearly a week as the local commander saw no point in firing the oil tanks when they were not under any immediate threat of capture. Tommy Goodwin had prudently arranged for a fishing boat to be moored off the refinery that was victualled with tinned food and water from the petrol depot. When it had been evacuated considerable quantities of supplies had been left behind.

Perhaps the Germans had overrun their administrative chain and were forced to pause here on the Seine or it may have been that they knew that the French were negotiating terms for a cease-fire, after which they would be able to move down the French coast without any opposition. After a week, a large contingent of French Marines who had been ready to defend Honfleur pulled out without telling anyone. At this point Goodwin was told that he could fire the tank farm and he did so immediately.

Here he made a fateful decision. He decided that rather than going by fishing boat, which would be very vulnerable to attack from the air, they would sneak down along the coastal road through Caen to St Nazaire. His hunch proved correct as they met no German patrols at all and arrived back intact at their destination.

Though the majority of the fighting troops of the British Expeditionary Force were taken off at Dunkirk, large numbers of troops on the lines of communication of the British Army and nearly all the RAF ground staff fell back mainly on St Nazaire. The major part played by the 'little ships' in the Dunkirk evacuation is well known. Large numbers of pleasure craft, sailing barges and the like went over to the beaches to ferry men home. The evacuation at St Nazaire was a completely different problem. It was many miles from England, round Ushant and down the Bay of Biscay coast. Here only seagoing ships could be used. The Ministry of War Transport at short notice got hold of every available ship to help; liners, tramp steamers, colliers and, indeed, any ship capable of making the journey. As there was no shortage of small boats such as tugs and trawlers at St Nazaire to ferry troops it was decided that all shipping taking part in the evacuation would anchor out to sea. At this time of year the North Atlantic was still very cold.

When they arrived at St Nazaire they were embarked on the old Cunarder *Lancastria* which, with the others, was lying at anchor outside the port and suffering random bombing from the German Air Force. The men were fed and then bedded down in a hold. The officers and senior NCOs were placed, as far as possible, in cabins. The ship had been converted into a troopship with a capacity of 3,000 passengers. In the event because of the urgency of the situation the captain took on about 6,500 of which nearly 1,000 were civilian refugees. Suddenly there was a concerted attack by five Dornier bombers just as the ship was about to weigh anchor. The first bomb exploded in the number two hold in which there were around 800 RAF personnel. Another bomb went straight down the funnel which proved fatal to the ship. She began to settle and in a few minutes rolled over and sank rapidly. Of the 6,500 souls on board there were less than 2,500 survivors. Lance Sergeant Ward vividly described what happened next:

*At about 3.15 p.m. we were awakened by alarm bells and we picked up the life jackets we found in the cabin and went out into the corridor which was full of senior NCOs and officers. Suddenly there was a distinctive crump and the ship began to list. Still no orders were issued, except by an American woman in uniform asking us to stand aside for women and children refugees, which we did.*

*We filed slowly out onto the deck, where I checked the lifeboats but found them lashed down and the turnbuckles rusted up. The ship was listing by then and some men were already in the water, which was being covered with oil. We could see an enemy plane still flying around the convoy but a destroyer thought to be HMS Highlander was sending up ack-ack and it was not possible to identify her positively. I can remember a soldier with a Bren gun on a mounting, maintaining fire until his tripod slipped over on the sloping deck. As the angle of list increased, I too decided to abandon ship and went over the side down a rope. I swam as hard as I could to get clear of the ship, and then trod water to decide my next move. I then found out why I was not so buoyant as usual – I was still wearing my steel helmet which I promptly jettisoned. I then heard somebody calling my name and found Lieutenant Whitehead and another man, who was not wearing a life jacket. I joined them and was asked to remove Lieutenant Whitehead's trousers. This I achieved with some difficulty as he was wearing both belt and braces and still had his jack knife on a lanyard around his waist. We looked around, and decided to swim to a French fishing boat that was picking up survivors. I swam on my back with my right hand supporting the third man who could not swim. Lieutenant Whitehead acted as navigator and helped push us along.*

*I had a good view of the ship and also saw bombs drop into the sea near a destroyer. The ship turned right over, with men walking and sitting on her bottom. I could also hear survivors singing 'Roll out the barrel' and 'There will always be an England'. When the ship was going under, we stopped swimming to allow Lieutenant Whitehead to see her go under. 'I take a poor view of that' was his comment.*

*After about an hour in the water, we eventually arrived at a French fishing craft where we were taken aboard. We were on this boat for some time, and the fit survivors were kept busy taking others up from the water. We tried artificial respiration on some bodies, but unfortunately, without success but it did serve to keep us warm. Early in the evening, we were all transferred to the SS* Cronsay, *which had also received a partial hit, which damaged her bridge and navigation equipment.*

Goodwin, who was a strong swimmer and Sapper Mitchell were also picked up so eventually four of them returned to England; Goodwin, Whitehead, Ward and Sapper Mitchell. It was very sad that, having volunteered for yet another task, the others should have perished on the *Lancastria*.

Chapter Seven

# DUNKIRK, CALAIS
# AND BOULOGNE

After we had deployed most of the unit onto the oil stocks on the Seine basin, Military Operations felt that it was perhaps worth tackling the smaller oil stocks at Dunkirk, Calais and Boulogne. The rear party at Gravesend, under Captain Bert West, was asked to provide sufficient sections to carry out these tasks. Not only did they leave Gravesend some time after we had left for France but they all returned before we did. On 23 May a section set off to Dunkirk on the destroyer *Wild Swan* with a naval demolition party. Bert West was in command of this section with Lieutenant Cyril Cox and about twenty other ranks. Commander Banks was in overall command of the combined demolition parties.

The situation, during these momentous days at Dunkirk, is vividly described by Cyril Cox:

*As Wild Swan approached Dunkirk a dense volume of black smoke could be seen ascending into the air. A quick inspection through field glasses revealed an oil installation blazing furiously. West looked at Cox trying in vain to hide the chagrin he felt, but a further investigation led to the discovery of about twenty tanks close to the shore so far safe and sound. This was reassuring, and it was an eager and confident band of sailors and sappers that Wild Swan carried rapidly past a burning oil tanker and the forlorn wrecks of two destroyers and various other craft that surrounded the narrow entrance channel into Dunkirk. As the destroyer berthed along side the shattered quay, the rain came down in*

69

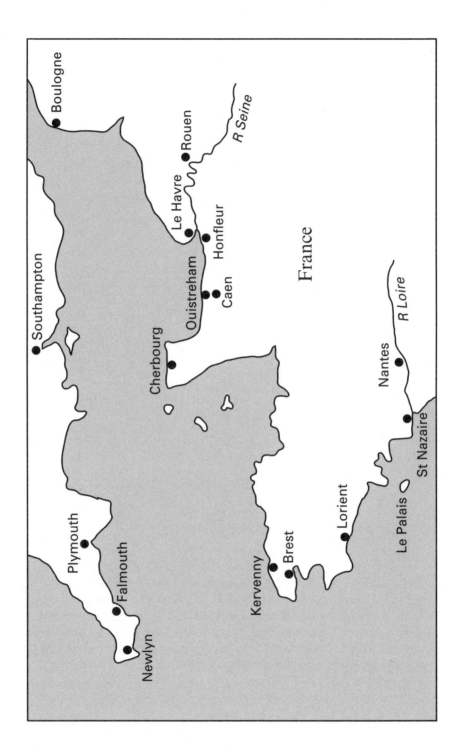

Boulogne

Rouen

R Seine

Le Havre

Honfleur

France

Southampton

Ouistreham

Caen

R Loire

Cherbourg

Nantes

Plymouth

Lorient

St Nazaire

Falmouth

Kervenny

Brest

Le Palais

Newlyn

*torrents and the poor visibility gave promise that the landing
would be uneventful – but within five minutes the destroyer's ack-
ack guns roared forth and the sappers had their baptism lying in
puddles of water.*

*West and Banks after explaining their mission were told to find
themselves billets in Malo-les-Bains and 'For Gods sake get these
explosives off the quay'. Luck was in for the ground staff of a
departing RAF squadron were only too pleased to get rid of their
lorries, and with two deserted refugees' cars, transport was assured.
About three hours after landing quite a respectable convoy of two
cars and five 3ton lorries moved away from the docks. Not a bad
start!*

*. . . it was a beautiful day with light fleecy clouds, ideal for
bombing and soon all three varieties, high, low and dive, were
going on fairly continuously. West had a lucky escape when one
side of his car was splintered as he got out of the other! About
midday, a phenomenon occurred which has since become common
place. A lone plane was seen describing a pretty white smoke ring
in the sky, and as the men stood watching what he was up to,
between fifty and sixty planes dived through and released their
load. The air was filled with whistles and crashes, dense clouds of
dust floated by, hardly had the first salvo ceased echoing when
again the planes came through on their second run up; bricks and
shrapnel flew about and the sappers and sailors were smothered in
dust and rubble, all with 10 tons of TNT within a few yards – as a
matter of fact some of the lads crawled under the laden lorries for
cover! When eventually the noise and dust subsided, both sides of
the street were quite flat and craters blocked the ends, but the
hundred yards of road the party occupied were untouched, and the
only casualties were one sailor badly bomb shocked and several
cuts and bruises from flying debris.*

*A strange change came over the town during the day; when the
party landed there was no organization or control, traffic went
where it liked, crowds of unarmed French soldiers wandered about,
officers, wounded or men who had lost their units milled around
HQ awaiting instructions, everything was chaotic. Then as the
British Army retired towards Dunkirk a few redcaps appeared and
order came with them; ack-ack guns and men arrived and raced to
take up positions to offer some opposition to the bombers. The ack-
ack gunners were magnificent, it was hard to believe that men could
become so weary and still keep going, each gun had only one team*

*– sometimes less than one – but still they kept pegging away twenty-four hours a day.*

*By now the town was ablaze, order was unobtainable and food supplies were running out, streams of ambulances and Red Cross trains came onto the shattered quay, many peppered with machine gun bullets and shrapnel gashes, whilst the VADs and RAMC laboured unceasingly with their merciful tasks, hospital ship after hospital ship being loaded despite machine gunning and bombing and dispatched to safer waters.*

*Next day it became obvious that the destruction of the oil storage tanks was unnecessary. The leaping flames and great volumes of smoke bore evidence that the enemy's bombs had found their mark, and Captain West placed his party at the disposal of the Commander RN. That day charges were placed in locks and cranes and by the evening all was ready, and the demolition party retired to a lighthouse, where, wonder of wonders water was obtainable from a well. Thirsts were slaked and empty water bottles refilled – a real piece of good luck.*

*One fact began to make itself obvious. Before long the quays and docks would become untenable, the Hun had the range only too well and knew just when to release his bombs to hit the target. It must have been about this time that the decision to use the beaches was taken and the necessary preparations set in hand.*

*Next day the first of the British Army began to arrive, and it was great to see the high spirits of the men tired as they were, and that every man still carried his weapon; there was no demoralisation here, everything seemed orderly and correct, at any rate at that early time.*

*Later that day Commander Banks decided that owing to the shortage of food and water the RE party should be evacuated right away. He refused to consider their eagerness to remain and assist him and sent them aboard a small drifter already packed solid with men. Hardly was the drifter ready to move away when down came three Messerschmitts and sprayed them with machine gun fire. Slowly the little ship gathered way and left the shattered town of Dunkirk, the flames of a hundred fires leaping skywards with the smoke joining into a black pall overhead. As they steamed towards England the watchers on the ship could see relays of bombers flying in over the smoke clouds and hear the roar of exploding bombs.*

As Bert West succinctly put it after they returned:

*The position was somewhat ludicrous. We were busy trying to destroy the oil stocks to prevent the Germans getting them. The Germans were bombing them to prevent the French and ourselves getting them and the French Fire Brigades were trying to put out the fires started by the German bombs!*

At the same time as the Dunkirk venture another section under Second Lieutenant Arthur Barton was sent to Calais. This was a disappointing job as the party was unable to get anywhere near to the oil tanks because there was heavy fighting already taking place. Fortunately the amount of fuel involved at the tank farm was not great. The party returned safely to Dover.

Another party was sent to Boulogne under Captain Bernard Buxton. When they arrived there was heavy fighting just outside the port. The intelligence was wrong as there were no oil stocks. At this stage the destroyers that came in were only taking off casualties. The party helped to prepare two bridges on the actual approaches to the harbour for demolition. They were continually bombed, shelled and every now and then they came under sniper and machine-gun fire. Sadly Sapper Wells was very badly wounded. The French doctors did what they could for him in the First Aid post on the quay and he was evacuated by destroyer but died on the way to Dover. The party eventually got away on one of the last destroyers able to get into the port.

During the last twenty-four hours of the evacuation at Boulogne no less than fifteen destroyers came and went absolutely packed with troops. On one of these trips a destroyer was lying alongside the quay taking on exhausted soldiers when four German tanks came almost down to the quay. The crews on the destroyer with their 4.7-inch guns were 'closed up' for action against air attack. In a moment the ships' guns engaged the tanks. The first shell missed, the second hit the first tank, ricocheted off, hitting the second tank and both were knocked out. The third shell hit the third tank fair and square and blew it to pieces and the fourth tank beat it.

This operation at Boulogne was officially described as abortive but Bernard Buxton summed it up well:

*The blokes were all grand, all nine of them, and at least they had swapped shots with Jerry at one hundred and fifty yards range and may have killed some – who knows?'*

Chapter Eight

# CHERBOURG AND ST MALO

The collapse of French resistance meant that XD operations, as these demolition operations were officially known, were no longer pre-planned but being mounted on an ad hoc basis. The four parties had returned from their operations at Dunkirk, Calais and Boulogne, before we got back from France. The operations had been abortive but only either because oil was non-existent or already destroyed by enemy action. The situation they found was well described by Cyril Cox, who was just back from Dunkirk, in his report:

*We arrived in Milton barracks with our natural elation clouded by the loss of one of our number, but at least confident of a warm welcome from the comrades we had left behind. Like a cold douche came reality, the bleak empty barracks with only a few familiar faces, cooks, waiters, telephonists and the like, the remainder of the unit had departed for the Havre-Rouen area. A strange Colonel sat in OC Troops Office and grudgingly granted each man twenty fours leave – most of it utilized to make up arrears of sleep – then set them to work on road blocks, sweeping the barracks, cleaning latrines and similar routine jobs. Captain West became Officer I/C road blocks. Captain Buxton accommodation Officer, Second Lieutenant Barton a sort of stores clerk and myself, a glorified office boy entitled Assistant Adjutant to OC Troops – a post which entailed sitting in the gloomy twilight of OC Troops office for about twelve hours each day. The comparison was too great for immediate adjustment of the human mind from the tense excitement of those hours under enemy fire to the quiet monotonous existence in barracks, and tempers became frayed, the men longed for a further smack at the common enemy, us two subalterns chaffed at the futility of our present occupation, and confided to each other our intense desire to escape from the soul destroying deadness, but the time passed slowly by and there seemed no prospect of relief.*

*At about 1.00 p.m. on Sunday, 6 June, I was sitting in the OC Troops Office signing 'for Adjutant', when the phone rang and a voice asked for Captain West saying 'Major Bourne here'. At the sound of that magic name I pricked up my ears and explained that Captain West was out but that I was the senior Kent Fortress officer in the barracks. 'Tell Captain West I want to know how many special parties he can form, and that I shall want about five parties at short notice'.*

Major Bourne was known to be a staff officer in Military Operations at the War Office so there was much excitement among all ranks at the prospect of release from this humdrum existence and the chance to get involved in further operations.

Oil storage installations at Caen, Cherbourg and St Malo were the objectives this time. One difficulty was that Caen was inland and the nearest port was Cherbourg eighty miles away. For this reason West decided to send a third officer to Cherbourg. The parties for Cherbourg and Caen were commanded by Lieutenant Cox with Second Lieutenants Barton and Birley, the latter having been specially posted in from Chatham at short notice. When they arrived at Portsmouth they were immediately embarked on HMS *Alresford*, a roomy ship which had been used previously as a navigation school. An hour later a naval demolition party arrived and both parties were put under command of Lieutenant Commander Grindle. They immediately put to sea and the Navy with their usual hospitality supplied the men with cocoa and bread and cheese and the officers enjoyed a meal in the wardroom. Everybody then turned in to get what sleep they could.

At 4.00 a.m. they were roused and the Navy again turned up trumps and gave them an excellent breakfast of bacon and eggs. An hour later they berthed alongside the *Gare Maritime* in Cherbourg. Grindle and Cox went to the British HQ that was close by in the local casino. Their arrival was completely unexpected and at first they were refused any sort of cooperation. After some time a sleepy naval liaison officer and an army staff officer were dug out of bed and it was learnt that the entire staff moved out to a château at night to avoid the routine bombing of the harbour. Cox managed, after much wrangling, to extract two 30cwt lorries and a four-seater car from them and also got reluctant permission to use the army huts near the harbour as billets for both parties. The news that the huts had been evacuated owing to the severity of the bombing attacks worried the chaps not at all! The OC of a local transit camp undertook to keep the men supplied with food and also lent them two cooks to prepare it.

When Grindle and Cox went to the local French naval authorities to discuss arrangements for the demolition of the oil, it was the usual story: 'It was absurd. The Germans could never advance so far, ridiculous, mad Englishmen!' It was evident that relations with the French had completely broken down. Grindle also complained that it was impossible to find who was in charge in the army; it appeared to be the most senior officer present but as he changed every few hours it made it very difficult to get a decision.

After a long argument Cox, with one party, was allowed to proceed to Ouistreham which was about eight miles south of Caen on the coast. Barton's party loaded their stores onto a lorry, with Cox and Barton in the car and proceeded to Caen. They were surprised at first to see signs saying 'Rue Bombe' but they realized after a mile or two it was merely to indicate a rough surface! The lorry broke down and after repairing it they eventually reached Caen where Barton was put in the hands of a French naval liaison officer and Cox returned by car to Cherbourg. There he found very little progress had been made in persuading the French to cooperate. Surprisingly Arthur Barton rang up to say that he had been allowed to destroy the oil stocks at Ouistreham but as his lorry was on its last legs, wanted another be sent for them. As Cox was achieving very little at Cherbourg he decided to go himself with a car, a lorry and a dispatch rider. Unfortunately the roads were being strafed and he first lost the motor cycle with a bullet through the engine, then the lorry was shot up through the back axle and so they were forced to return when only about three miles from Caen. It subsequently transpired that the Germans were already in Caen. Cox telephoned Barton at Ouistreham through the Caen exchange, telling him to get back as best he could using country roads. They managed to patch up their broken down lorry and, by hugging back roads, reached Cherbourg safely some three hours later.

All the fuel stored at Cherbourg was bunker oil and Cox realized that it would be virtually impossible to destroy quickly as the tanks were all underground and no oxygen would be available. However they were unable even to try as the French naval guards prevented their entry to the site right to the end.

Commander Grindle then instructed Cox to join in the port demolitions which they did, with relish. Cranes were toppled over into the dock, ships were sunk and one outstanding feature was the felling of a pair of 250-ton sheer legs which took a 2,000-ton coaster to the bottom with them. At the last moment they all ran onto HM destroyer *Sabre* which was moored stern on to the quay and as the last man jumped on, it took off like a scalded cat.

The section bound for St Malo was under the command of Second Lieutenant Ashwell. When they arrived at Portsmouth they embarked on HMS *Wild Swan*. Sapper Shelton gives an apt description:

> On arrival at Portsmouth we were greeted with some very choice language from the naval ratings to go on the job with us. They had been with us on other raids and that accounted for their greeting!

After a meal, they set sail and stopped briefly at Jersey in the Channel Islands where some officers went ashore before pushing on to St Malo, where they disembarked. Sapper Shelton takes up the story again:

> After disembarking we made our way to the casino, where we were to be billeted during our stay. We were put in the picture by Lieutenant Ashwell, after which we took up positions on road blocks. At that time troops were marching back from Rennes and embarking for England. We saw the last troops go and the last boat. Our worry was how we were to get out when our job was completed. After several days we were told by Lieutenant Ashwell

*that the Germans were at Rennes and it was time to get cracking. Our work was to be a tank farm, and very awkward it proved, owing to the fact that in front of the storage tanks were a row of houses.*

*After smashing the valves and opening the cocks to flood all round the tanks, and with all our men accounted for, Lieutenant Ashwell fired his Very pistol to complete the job. Another successful mission.*

*We made for the harbour and to our surprise and relief found about six motor boats waiting for us. We afterwards found out that the arrangements had been made by those officers who went ashore at Jersey for a group of very brave volunteers to bring us out of St Malo. We were very relieved to be out of France.*

*After a very rough trip we arrived at St Helier, all glad to be on dry land once more. We spent two days in St Helier and enjoyed a good rest and we then received orders to move on as the Germans had occupied St Malo. We left St Helier on the only boat available, the SS Rye, which was loaded with potatoes, and after a hectic voyage we landed at Weymouth. Another exercise successfully completed.*

*We owe our sincere thanks to the brave men of St Helier.*

## Chapter Nine

# ROBINSON CRUSOE – BREST

On 16 June while we were still away on the Seine, West, who was commanding the rear party at Gravesend, was rung by Military Operations at the War Office to say that the situation in France was deteriorating so fast and that more demolition teams were needed. As only Bert West and Bernard Buxton were in barracks with the residue of the unit of half a dozen sappers, West said,

'Buxton and I will have to go'. But wisely West was ordered to stay at Gravesend to keep continuity. It was explained to the War Office that Don Terry's party from the Seine who, you will remember had been evacuated earlier by destroyer to England, were on leave. West said that he should be able to raise the three officers and thirty men required by the morning. This was only possible as being a Territorial unit nearly all the men lived in Northfleet and Gravesend. The six sappers who were in barracks spent the evening going round the two towns knocking up their mates for another 'party'.

The next morning as requested, Buxton reported to the War Office for instructions while West took all the rest of the party to Waterloo Station, as had been ordered the previous evening, complete with their usual arms, preserved rations, morphine tablets and other miscellaneous impedimenta by now common-place to these jobs as section stores. Here they boarded the train to Plymouth and a very disappointed West waved them off and returned to Gravesend where he and an elderly batman were all that was left in the unit lines. There were three sections of ten men each, with Buxton, Terry and Second Lieutenant Owens as the three officers.

When they arrived at Devonport they were shown onto HMS *Cutty Sark*. This ship had originally been built as a destroyer at the end of the Great War but had been acquired by the Duke of Westminster as a yacht. The cabins were fragrantly scented and luxuriously furnished. She had been requisitioned by the Navy in 1939. Remarkably for one of HM's ships and to the sappers' horror there was not a drop of drink on board!

They sailed from Devonport at midnight on the night of the 17–18 June and arrived off Ushant at about 9.00 a.m. They proceeded into the Anse de Berthaume, just inside the entrance of the long channel up to Brest. They tied up alongside HM destroyer *Broke*. Here two of the sections under Buxton were transferred to *Broke* to move on into Brest.

Meanwhile Terry with his section headed off to Lorient in *Cutty Sark*. Terry had just sat down to lunch when she was bombed and hit. Don Terry got no lunch as the galley aft was hit and more importantly the steering gear was irreparably damaged. During the remaining period of daylight they were drifting helplessly and feeling extremely vulnerable. The next morning a British destroyer took her in tow and they arrived back at Devonport that evening.

Thirty-six hours later they put to sea again in HM destroyer *Vanquisher* and twelve hours later they arrived off Le Palais. They and the naval demolition party were under the command of Commander Sherbrook. Here they went ashore and found there were no suitable demolition targets so they then re-embarked. *Vanquisher* joined another destroyer and they carried out anti U-boat sweeps in the Bay of Biscay during rough weather which was quite an experience for the sappers. As the destroyers were getting short of fuel they returned to Devonport.

Meanwhile Bernard Buxton and the two sections on *Broke* who, with the naval demolition party, were under the command of Commander Sir G. Congrieve, moved off to Brest. Congrieve was a formidable character with a large black beard who insisted on wearing army battledress.

Steaming into Brest they passed the French Atlantic Fleet and docked near the Admiralty Quay. The naval and military officers spent the afternoon in conference with the French admiral and his staff, a delicate, difficult and tedious undertaking. They were told that the Germans were not expected to reach Brest before noon on the following day at the earliest. After all, one can fully appreciate the misgivings of the French authorities and their desire to put off the final demolitions until the last possible moment, for once the job was done it was irrevocable. Furthermore, any demolition of this nature needs careful consideration and planning to avoid hampering offensive action or the withdrawal of the defenders. Moreover, these elderly officers of high rank, often recalled from retirement, had a sublime optimism. One could detect their disbelief in the probability of the enemy actually arriving at the gates and battering their way through. I suppose this false sense of security is infectious for more often than not their staff seemed to reflect the same outlook.

While this long drawn out session was in progress the party unloaded stores. One officer with a small party did a hasty reconnaissance in the area to locate the targets. Astonishingly people were still shopping; a large department store was crowded; cafes were full and girls were riding about on bicycles.

The French admiral, who was preoccupied with getting the French Fleet to sea before the Germans arrived, did agree to the sappers preparing the oil installations for demolition but on the firm understanding that they would only be fired on his authority. There were four oil storage sites at Brest. Five of the sappers were sent off with a naval demolition party some way from the main dockyard. These men were not seen again until the main body had returned to Gravesend. The main storage sight had a high fence round it with a guard at the gate who refused to let them in. So they had to go back to the admiral's office which was some way away in the town. To reach this they had to cross the harbour by motorboat, all of which was time consuming. At this point the admiral attached a French naval liaison officer to Buxton to assist them. On the way back Buxton met Commander McKye RN, who was the British liaison officer with the French Atlantic Fleet. McKye stressed the importance of not firing the oil tanks until authorized by the French admiral. He felt that the relationship with our French Allies was in such a

82

delicate state that destroying the oil without orders would irreparably damage the situation.

The tanks at the main site were of the usual size of 120 feet across and 50 feet high but unusually they were sunk into the ground so that the tops were below ground level. There was the usual bund which in this case was rather like a dry moat around the tanks. Access to the tanks was down a spiral steel staircase. There were two further problems. The admiral had insisted that no explosives were to be used prior to the general order for destruction: the implication of this was that spanners had to be found and the sappers had the laborious business of undoing pipe flanges to let some fuel out instead of blowing off the valves which had become their normal practice. In addition, as it was a dockyard, nearly all the fuel was bunker oil that was time consuming to fire using blankets soaked in kerosene. About this time, the French Navy brought no less than eight tons of cheddite to one of the sites thinking it might help. In fact this explosive was of no use to the sappers anyhow. Cheddite had a very poor reputation for stability.

Congrieve found Buxton and brought him and the men some food. Buxton told Congrieve of his conversation with Commander McKye and his deep reservations about firing the fuel without the admiral's consent. Congrieve's reply was decisive. As far as he was concerned, the job was going up, French or no French, and he had come to France for a party and was damn well going to have one! He said that the destroyer could not wait in Brest because the risk was too great but she would withdraw seawards to the Anse de Bethaume. He also attached a naval rating to them, complete with a motorboat he had got hold of, to enable the sapper party to make their way out of the port to RV with the destroyer waiting ten to fifteen miles out.

A French naval officer who spoke a little broken English, came up and said, very excitedly 'Light de fire – Et is most urgent'. Fortunately this was just before Buxton and his chaps were going to start anyway. The task went fairly well. The flaming blankets were gently dropped onto the oil and after a period of suspense the fire gradually got away but once started, the flames went well over the top of the tanks. As each group got their number of tanks away the sappers were sent off down to the motorboat. Inevitably some tanks took longer than others. One was particularly difficult and by the time it was alight, the ones on their exit route were well and truly away and Buxton and two others had a hot and singeing sprint to get clear!

When they had all arrived on the quay they set out in the motorboat with the naval rating to find the destroyer *Broke*. Just as they thought they were clear of the harbour entrance, the engine spluttered to a halt. They were left drifting helplessly until they managed to attract the attention of two French sailors also in a motorboat by firing revolver shots into the air. In hesitant French the situation was explained and the two sailors agreed to take them out to the destroyer which was lying some miles out to seawards. Shortly after they were underway they got caught up in the harbour boom defences. It took them a little while to disentangle themselves and find the exit. The flames from the fires were reflected in the harbour and far out to sea, colouring the whole bay with a dull orange hue. As they were making their way seawards and gazing back in silence at the fires there was a sudden terrific detonation. As one man everyone murmured, 'Cheddite'.

The motorboat was now over five miles out from Brest and would shortly be entering the Anse de Bethaume. At this stage the smoke had become thinner and visibility was improving. When they got into the bay they found it deserted. They circled right round to be certain but there was no sign of *Broke* or any other ship. Clearly a decision had to be made quickly. They were about 160 miles from the nearest point in England – the Lizard. The naval rating, now part of their group, reckoned that the motorboat was making ten knots. The time was currently 2.30 a.m. Their dilemma was whether to wait for the destroyer which might, of course, already be on its way to England or to head for England on their own and hope that a destroyer would either catch them up or come back and look for them. What was surprising was that there was no sign of either the naval demolition party or Commander Congrieve, who were also meant to be at the RV.

Buxton decided to head for England. They headed due west to

give them sea room before turning due north for England. Strangely the two French sailors, one of whom was still on the helm, never so much as questioned the order to head out to sea!

All went well for some hours, relatively speaking of course, as it was blowing hard with a fairly heavy sea running. They were seasick with the continuous heavy rolling of the boat and a not very effective crew to cope with the difficult situation. Daybreak found them out of sight of land still plugging along northwards with the sea increasing and the great majority of them lying in the bilge too sick to care what happened. At 5.30 a.m. the engine started to splutter and then failed altogether. They drifted along before the wind broadside on and wallowing in the rough sea. At this time they thought they were half way to England. After some time the cause of the engine failure was traced to a blocked fuel pipe, probably due to the heavy rolling of the boat disturbing detritus at the bottom of the fuel tank. As one of the party said afterwards, he could not understand how a gravity feed could work at all when 'most of the time the ruddy boat was on its beam ends'. Having cleared the offending fuel feed pipe they tried to start up again, but after a few minutes the starting gear gave up the ghost. They now realized that they were up against fate for the wind was approaching gale force and with seas running high, it looked as if the end was not far off. Only three of the crew were capable of any exertion, the remainder being completely down and out with sickness and exposure. Everybody was soaked to the skin. Those still able to take any interest in life at all realized that with the increasing sea the launch must inevitably turn over, or at least, be swamped, unless they could keep her head up. They rigged up a small jib with a groundsheet and this proved just sufficient to do this. To this they probably owe their lives. So it was that from early morning on Wednesday until Thursday afternoon, they were at the mercy of the elements and feeling very sorry for themselves. During this time they had traversed a wide circle, first into mid channel and then back to France.

On Thursday afternoon they sighted the rocky cliffs of the Brittany Coast. A white house on the top of a prominent headland had been visible for sometime before they actually saw land.

There was little to be done in the way of navigation as they dared not alter course for fear of capsizing, so they ran before the wind which fortunately seemed to be taking them straight for the coast. As the boat got nearer to the coast they saw many large rocks between them and what appeared to be a sandy bay at the foot of the cliffs. The heavy seas were breaking over these isolated rocks with considerable violence, sending clouds of white foam and spray high into the air with each succeeding wave.

The three members of the party who were still on their feet looked out upon what they were convinced would be their end. They could not rouse the remainder of the occupants sufficiently to get them to take any interest in the prospect of being ship-wrecked on a lee shore. Furthermore as the sandy bay, then clearly discernible, was the best part of a mile beyond the first rocks, their physical condition put any ideas of swimming out of the question.

They went scudding along towards the shore quite powerless to prevent the inevitable disaster. However fate had the whole thing planned and all they could do was wait. They could now see fishing boats drawn up on the beach, an occasional cottage or two and fishing nets spread out on the beach. It seemed a perverse state of affairs to have got so near to land again after the recurring dangers of the previous few days, and to have their hopes banished by the rocks just ahead. As they approached the shore they found that an increasing swirl of the flowing tide drew them, as if in a maelstrom away from the rocks, and they shot past in a channel between two rocky islets. On they went towards the shore swirling first one way then another, completely out of control and more often than not, broadside on to the larger rocks in the bay. Then a fisherman, who had seen their predicament, put out to their rescue. Sailing his little craft with great skill near to the derelict launch, he got a line across and towed them into quiet water and, taking a number of the party into his boat, sailed inshore. It took several trips, but in time all were taken off and laid out on the beach by the Breton fisher folk who by then had gathered around. In spite of their physical condition, in some cases bordering on collapse, after an hour or so stretched out in the warm sun, and after the village women had brought them hot coffee, they regained sufficient interest in life to sit up and ask where they were. They had in fact landed at the small Breton fishing village of Kervenny. They had had no food for nearly three days, but at this stage, they were too far gone to eat.

After they had been on land about two hours the village *curé* appeared on the scene and took matters in hand. He was a kindly old soul, with white hair, ascetic features and a demeanour which simply radiated goodwill upon these weary British soldiers. He spoke little English, but strangely enough wrote it well, so with pencil and paper this old priest explained the position to the leader of the party. It appeared that the Germans were only a few miles away and were approaching the village. He offered to help them if they would throw all their uniforms and warlike equipment into the sea, put on clothes he would provide and proceed immediately to a hiding place. These conditions were accepted and in a short time the good fisher folk raked up enough spare clothing to rig out the whole party as Bretons. One of the fishermen took their uniforms and equipment out to sea and dumped them, so scared were they that the Germans might find it during the inevitable search when they entered the village. These simple people were under no illusion as to the fate of all concerned if they were caught harbouring our men.

The British put on their newly acquired miscellaneous garments, in the main bell bottomed fishermen's trousers, with highly coloured shirts and scarves to complete their disguise. Women's jumpers sometimes replaced the shirts and one lad, in lieu of trousers was handed a pair of women's extra, outsize bloomers which hung down round his ankles in the most whimsical manner. His quaint appearance clearly indicated that the Breton woman must have been very large in proportions. When rigged out, the whole party would have graced any theatrical performance as stage bandits. The hospitable fishing folk gave them two or three loaves and a bottle of wine and promised more, should it be possible after the enemy had arrived.

Without delay they moved off with the padre who led them along the shore and after turning up his trousers waded through the ebbing tide towards an island out in the bay. They went in single file, following the guide, who picked his way with care, for it appeared to be a natural causeway never completely uncovered by the sea, but safe to those who knew its direction. Some thousand yards out from the beach they came to the shore of the island; their guide said goodbye and returned to the mainland leaving the weary shipwrecked young men to clamber up the cliff and survey the setting of the next phase of their adventures.

Having scrambled to the top, they looked upon an undulating field about 100 yards wide and possibly 400 yards long. Some attempt at cultivation was in evidence for in one corner of the area the remains of a carrot crop was noticed. Over at the end facing the mainland was a small cottage with the conventional water butt under the eaves. A lean-to shed completed the minute homestead. A few decrepit hens clustered under the lee side to escape the wind that, while abating, was still blowing half a gale.

Making their way to the cottage, they knocked on the door but there was no reply. They thought perhaps the occupants were at the back of the building although, in view of its smallness, it seemed odd that they had not been heard. Perhaps the wind had prevented the occupants hearing? The explorers went round to the other side but again drew a blank; an aged and scraggy cow was seen through the open door of the shed; this at least reassured them of human occupation. After a further wait, a shower of rain prompted them to push open the door of the little cottage, and one by one they crowded inside to seek sanctuary from the bleak weather outside. The place was deserted. There were two little rooms in the cottage, one a living room and one about the size of a large packing case, was obviously the bedroom as it contained two wooden bunks covered with mattresses. In the living room were two chairs, a table and a fireplace in which were ashes. On the rough mantel shelf were a few tin canisters, a crucifix and a broken fragment of mirror. That completed the picture except for an absurdly small window which overlooked the bay and through which could be seen the lighthouse and cottages just above the beach.

When the rain abated sufficiently, Buxton surveyed the shore with his field glasses which, with a prismatic compass, were all they had salvaged of war equipment. 'Come here Owens' he called to the subaltern, 'see if you can see what I can see'. Sure enough, the Germans were entering the village. All eyes strained to get a glimpse through the restricted opening. Yes, there was no doubt about those grey-green uniforms and, if further proof had been needed, soon afterwards the swastika was hoisted on the signal staff on the cliff.

They held a council of war, and plans were made to avoid detection or other complications. The cottage had obviously been lived in fairly recently, as witness a little ground coffee in one of the tins, the chicken and the cow who was in milk but without calf. The conclusion they came to was that their good friend the priest had arranged for the former occupants to leave the island and that their good fortune was part of his plan for succour.

After these deliberations, which seemed to provide a satisfactory explanation for their newly found surroundings, consideration was given to an appreciation of the situation from a military point of view. They argued that the Germans being an unimaginative people would probably not put off in a boat to the island providing their suspicions were not aroused. All were agreed that the villagers would not incur the displeasure of 'his reverence' by giving the fugitives away. The last decision of this strange conference was that if the army of the Greater Reich <u>did</u> land on the island, there was nothing for it, as they were unarmed, but to surrender. In point of fact this last decision was subsequently amended, for after a night's sleep and a meal of carrots, they felt full of fight; an interesting point to be noted by the medical profession. The first standing order was to the effect that during daylight, never more than two would go outside the cottage at the same time and also that when in view of the beach, they should be going through the motions of hoeing carrots. This part of their plan was put into effect straight away by two of the men going out and gathering some sticks and lighting the fire on which they boiled freshly dug carrots giving them all a hot meal accompanied by a slice of bread apiece.

That night they slept soundly, packed like sardines, taking up every available square foot of floor area. It must be remembered that there were eighteen men all told squeezed into that little cottage; 'like the Black Hole of Calcutta' was the general opinion.

89

But, as the only alternative was to share the box-like shed with the cow or face certain capture, it had to be endured. The next morning the first two detailed for exercise wandered round the island and found a small plot of potatoes, a great stroke of luck as the question of eking out an existence with so many to feed was their most serious problem. For the first two days they had a slice of bread each, hot boiled potatoes and raw carrots, but after that the bread was finished. The wine was issued in microscopic tots but this too soon came to an end. The two chickens were laying most days, so they saved the eggs until all could have half an egg each. Occasionally at night, two Frenchmen would arrive covertly with a little food to help them to eke out their very limited food. This 'Robinson Crusoe' existence was endured for a whole week but by then they were getting despondent and didn't see much hope of escape. They tried to console each other with the fact that they had had a poor start, what with three days adrift in a gale and being driven ashore onto an enemy coast, otherwise their diet of carrots and potatoes would have been fine! As it was they were a haggard party mentally and physically.

Each day, all but the two out of doors, sat huddled up in the cottage. They maintained a duty watch through the little window and watched the Germans on the shore and steadily cursed them and all that they represented. They told stories to each other though even these had to be rationed to make them last as long as possible. They talked of families and relations, of work before the war and all the homely things they could think of to pass those long dreary days. At night their dreams were mainly about their time in that open boat wallowing in heavy seas. One lad who had been brought up on a farm tried to milk the cow, but as she only understood French, his entreaty to 'come on old girl' did not seem to convince her. After some perseverance, she relented and they got about a quart of milk after which she kicked the door off the shed to conclude the proceedings.

At the end of the week things looked serious, as the Hun had evidently come to stay. What had happened to their friend the padre was the main theme of conversation. They had grown beards by now and were beginning to wonder what a British soldier really looked like. One thing upon which they all agreed was that they could take a lot more yet, while the carrots lasted and providing they got rain soon enough to replenish their sadly depleted water butt. At the end of the week, one evening after dark, they were down at the cove bathing when a ghostly little fishing boat drew up onto the sands and grounded.

At first all were convinced that it was the Hun and, naked as they were, they surrounded the dark form which stepped ashore and were prepared to take him on. However it was a fisherman who had been sent out by the priest to negotiate the hire of a craft which would take them back to England. After much consultation this Frenchman agreed to bring a fishing smack and come out to them the following evening. The fare was to be 30,000 francs, payable in French currency when they arrived on the other side of the channel. Spirits rose tremendously, but the next day seemed like a life sentence. At last darkness fell and they assembled down at the little cove. Sure enough, before long the fishing boat came into sight and the fishermen, with the aid of their dinghy, ferried the whole party out. They were afloat once again.

The crew consisted of two grisly Bretons who, having supervised the stowage of their peculiar freight through the hatchway, brought her up into the wind and slid silently out from the bay setting course northwards. The channel crossing was a tedious affair, particularly during the day when the skipper insisted they must remain out of sight. Twice planes came down and looked the little craft over but flew off obviously uninterested.

After nineteen hours at sea they made a very fortunate landfall, for what turned out to be the Lizard was sighted on the starboard bow. They then made for Newlyn in Cornwall. When nearing the harbour a launch came out from the examination vessel and, circling cautiously round the party who were all on deck by now, hailed them. Coming alongside the naval officer bawled through a megaphone 'Who the hell are you?' A thickset but haggard little man with a beard, wearing wide bell bottomed blue trousers and a red striped shirt replied 'Captain Bernard Buxton, Royal Engineers'. What the navy said was not audible, which was perhaps as well.

Once ashore, the financial commitments were discharged, a

night in bed, a visit to the barber and then the return, still in the 'onion sellers' clothes to their unit in Gravesend.

So ended a fairly hectic two week adventure. The remarks of the Quarter Guard at the entrance to the barracks when the party sought admission, mirrored those of the naval examination officer at Penzance.

Chapter Ten

# IRAQ

In August 1940 we were ordered to send one of our more experienced officers to the War Office where he would be briefed and we were warned that he was likely to be away for some time.

Peter Keeble, who by now was a major, arrived at the Military Operations Branch in the War Office where he was put in the picture. The Government was most concerned about the Iraqi oilfields at Kirkuk which were British owned. It was considered that Hitler might decide to strike eastwards if only to secure oil supplies which his war machine so desperately needed. Because of our unit's experience in oil denial it was decided to send an officer out to the Middle East GHQ to advise them as soon as possible. This was Keeble's mission. Before leaving they asked him if there was anything they could do to help him and he asked them to type a letter of introduction for him which he could show to the authorities during his trip to ease his way through military bureaucracy. Keeble was then sent to the Movements Branch who were to arrange for his speedy transit to GHQ at Cairo.

The demolition of oil wells as distinct from oil tank farms and refineries was completely new ground for us. Keeble appreciated straight away that it is one thing to set fire to oil storage tanks but quite another to destroy oil wells. In slight desperation, after leaving the War Office, he went straight to Foyles bookshop and bought a book on the drilling and production of oil. This he studiously read during his journey to the Middle East but he found he was not much the wiser on how to destroy oil wells!

A day or two later he found himself boarding the liner *Windsor Castle* at Greenock on the Clyde. She was still very much as she

93

had been in peacetime and he was allocated a comfortable first class cabin. They set sail as part of a large convoy. What an impressive sight it was as it spread out over the surface of the ocean. The convoy's speed could be no more than the speed of the slowest tramp steamer, probably about eight knots. The next morning Keeble and the other passengers came on deck and to their amazement they looked out on an empty ocean with not a ship in sight. Later in the morning the captain of the ship spoke on the Tannoy system to all the passengers and told them that the convoy had been attacked by U-boats in the night and three of the merchantmen had been sunk. None of them had heard anything. The convoy commodore, a retired senior naval officer who had come back into the Service for the war, signalled the *Windsor Castle* after the attacks giving her captain the choice of either staying with the convoy or pulling out and making use of her vastly greater speed as a mail ship, to proceed on her own. He decided on the latter course of action. One of Keeble's fellow passengers was a senior gunner major with a DSO who General Wavell had asked for to help out in the planned Ethiopian campaign; he was Orde Wingate.

The rest of the voyage was uneventful and they docked in Cape Town three weeks later as, for obvious reasons, they had had to make a wide sweep out into the Atlantic and not gone by the normal direct route.

At Cape Town passengers of all ranks were picked up by families who had them to stay and entertained these strangers royally. This hospitality was repeated whenever visiting troop ships arrived by these very generous people of loyal British stock who lived at the Cape. Keeble and a few of his colleagues, including Orde Wingate, who were urgently needed in Cairo, went by train to Durban the next day. There they were transferred to an Imperial Airways flying boat, landing at Entebbe, Juba, Khartoum, Luxor and eventually Cairo. At all the intermediate stops they stayed the night in the best hotels in great comfort!

As soon as he had arrived Keeble reported to General Wavell's Chief of Staff who told him about the problems at Kirkuk. They, that is the Middle East Headquarters, were not sure of the probable effectiveness of their present plan to deal with the oil fields. The code name for this plan was 'Bullion'. Because of their concern they had discussed with the War Office the possibility of sending out an 'oil denial expert' from England. Keeble sensibly did not let on that he had no knowledge whatsoever of destroying oil wells.

He had been told before he left England to take civilian clothes with him and also his passport. However he was issued with a new additional passport so that when it was necessary to show it, there would be no clue as to where he had been. He left Cairo and was flown up to Haifa where he met the Chief Engineer of Palestine who was the sapper officer responsible for operations in Iraq at that time. He was then flown to Habbaniyah by the RAF. This RAF base went back to the 1920s and was built around a lake in Southern Iraq, miles from anywhere. They had, over the years, made it almost luxurious. One would not have known that there was a war on and life went on as normal. No blackout, cinemas, sailing on the lake and every comfort that could be expected. It had been developed as a staging post for India and the Far East. Not only aeroplanes could land there but also flying boats on the lake. However once outside the perimeter of the base there was nothing, just desert. No wonder so much effort had gone into making the base tolerable for the inmates who in pre-war days could be stationed there for years at a time.

Here Keeble's task had to become more clandestine. He changed into civilian clothes and the next day he was picked up by the British manager of the Kirkuk oilfield. He was flown up north to Kirkuk by the manager in his private plane. Here the manager and his wife kindly had him to stay during this period.

He was ably briefed by the manager who was not only a tower of strength but full of innovative ideas. Apparently there were no less than fifty-six oil wells belonging to the company in and around Kirkuk. The oil was pumped hundreds of miles across the desert to the refineries at Haifa in Palestine. Of the fifty-six oil wells all but three were shut down. With Italy having entered the war, tankers could no longer ply down the Mediterranean to take on oil. The three wells in current use were kept operating to supply our Eastern Mediterranean fleet.

The fifty-three oil wells not required had to be 'neutralized' somehow. Keeble suggested setting fire to them as an option only to be told by the Manager that they would burn all right but the flames could in time be snuffed out and the wells re-used. Eventually what they settled for was dropping the bottom section of the boring pipe with the hardened head for drilling uppermost down the well. They then back filled the well with concrete. This was all done with oil company labour. No demolition can ever be permanent but to make matters more difficult for the Axis forces should they ever overrun Iraq, the drilling rigs, which could easily be dismantled for moving from site to site, were sent south to Basra. Here they were taken out to sea and dumped. These measures would ensure that it would take the Axis forces many months before they could exploit the oil reserves. The manager was confident that he could handle the last three wells on his own if the situation should arise.

The next problem was how to deny the use of the pipeline to Haifa should it be necessary. There were several pumping stations at regular intervals along the pipeline. The oil company employed a retired Naval Commander who had been an engineer officer to keep these pumping stations working. Keeble found that he had already anticipated that these stations might have to be destroyed. He had adopted a most ingenious solution. The pumps were a considerable size. He had ordered a new crankshaft for the machinery in each pumping station. The new crankshafts had had a pocket machined out of the metal and high explosives had been inserted. There was also a pocket for a glass file of acid, fuse and detonator. Should the Axis ever get close to Iraq the crankshafts would be changed over and if it became necessary to destroy the plant the acid file would be broken, the machine run up to full speed and the crankshaft would then be shattered by the explosion. The heavy spinning flywheel would 'take off' destroying everything in its path.

They motored along the pipeline visiting all the pumping stations from Kirkuk to Haifa in a large open shooting brake with six of them on board. When they approached the Iraqi–Palestine border posts they suddenly realized that Keeble, who was posing as a civilian, was devoid of any entries in his passport as he had been flown into Habbaniyah by the RAF and not passed through immigration controls. The consensus of opinion in the car was that if all the passports, less Keeble's, were passed up to the passenger in the front seat, all would be well. The five other passports made quite a pile and the man at the Customs and Immigration never bothered to count them and the car was waved through! Back in Haifa Keeble reported to the chief engineer and told him what had been achieved and the plans that were in place in case of an Axis attack. He was then flown down to Cairo and gave the chief of staff a similar report

Keeble was now faced with getting home. Despite his relatively junior rank he had been given the highest priority on his journey out to the Middle East but he rated no such priority on his homeward trip. However his letter originating from the Director of Military Operations at the War Office acted like a magic wand in the Movements Branch at GHQ. In a day or two Keeble found himself boarding a small aeroplane. The few other passengers were all very senior service officers or important diplomats. After flying for hours over open desert they eventually landed at an airstrip in French Equatorial Africa where the aircraft was refuelled and they spent the night. The next day they flew on to Lagos. In due course Keeble again with the aid of his influential letter was able to board an Imperial Airways flying boat bound for England.

On the way back they landed at Freetown, Bathurst in the Gambia and Lisbon. Each night was spent as before in luxurious hotels so very different from wartime Britain. They eventually landed at Poole. Keeble had been away for nearly three months. He reported to Military Operations at the War office to debrief them and requested permission to return to his unit. They said 'Of course, however you do not know where they are; they have gone to Northern Ireland!'

## Chapter Eleven

# MICAWBERS ALL

After the fall of France we were quartered in Gravesend again on the south side of the River Thames between London and the estuary. It was inevitable that after these XD operations there was much discussion over what quantity of oil had actually been destroyed. By assessing the number of oil tanks and their rough capacity, the consensus of opinion was that nearly 2 million tons had been destroyed or in other words 450 – 500 million gallons of fuel.

Since our arrival in Gravesend earlier in the year we had been slowly expanding into Corps Troop Engineers which would ultimately consist of three army field companies of nearly 300 men each and a field park company of about 200 men. Over the summer of 1940 the Kent Fortress Engineers were gradually joined by the Suffolk Fortress Engineers TA, elements of the Cinque Ports Engineers TA and a complete London TA Field Park Company. As all these units were small, there was a further influx of sappers from the Training Battalions and, most usefully, some excellent young second lieutenants from the Royal Engineer Officer Training Unit.

We worked long hours on defences against the ever impending threat of invasion; it was pill boxes, weapon pits, slit trenches and road blocks ad infinitum. Barbed wire became like a bad dream, in fact it became such a large part of life that at times it seemed to overshadow life itself, aptly styled the 'barbed wire blues'! Everyone felt that the historic words of the Prime Minister were about to become true at any moment.

*We shall defend our island, whatever the cost may be, we shall fight on the beaches, we shall fight on the landing grounds, we shall fight in the fields, and in the streets, we shall fight in the hills; we shall never surrender.*

Defence schemes had by this time decentralized almost down to the local policeman, and digging in against the invader was contagious. Everybody was at it, day and night, particularly in south-east England; hence RE Field Companies were in high demand. Looking back, one wonders whether much of it would have been effective, but at least it kept the army busy in those dark days when Britain stood alone. The psychological effect was wholly beneficial. An occasional 'stand to' at first light, which turned tired and sleepy sappers out to man vulnerable points, was our only change of employment for some months. In the meantime we would, as a welcome relief to the rather dull daily round of hard work on defences, fall to discussing the prospects of another 'party' as, far from becoming 'defence minded', we looked forward to another operation.

Situated as we were on the approaches to London, air action above was not infrequent, but usually sporadic and not sustained. Life in our town seemed to go on much the same, ships went up and down the river, and in the country the folk worked in the fields. Then daylight raids began increasing, with rumours of fierce attacks on nearby fighter airfields. The news on the wireless was non-committal, if not wholly reassuring, and the demand for ground defences gave way to demands for shelters and other protective works against bombing. Finally, the Luftwaffe put in several successive daylight attacks culminating in attacks in great strength, which subsequently became known as the Battle of Britain.

Working below, it was our good fortune to witness this epic fight; a spectacle never to be forgotten, even amongst the vicissitudes of a world war. In a clear sky high up above, layer upon layer of bombers all keeping perfect formation came out of the east, and droned steadily westwards towards the capital. With the sun glinting upon them, their regular formation gave the impression of the keyboard of some mammoth organ in the sky.

All heads were turned upwards; the men leaning on their shovels rested from their task and were spellbound by the moving panorama which was unfolding above. Then our fighters, all too few it seemed, roared into action with their familiar high pitched whine. This had little effect at first, and the vast armada moved overhead from the east into the west towards the capital. Then a few trails of smoke and gaps in the formation showed at least that the 'Jerries' were not going unscathed. At this stage more of our fighters joined the mêlée having been vectored in by Fighter Command. Then the smoky trails of falling aircraft increased and large gaps were discernible in the formation until the whole array broke up and not infrequently turned for home. As one lad said when he broke the silence 'the bastards can't take it', which just about summed up the situation.

After a brief lull, night bombing of London became the vogue, and in common with most of England we spent the nights in shelters. With enemy bombers groaning overhead, we sat drowsily packed in, listening to the ack-ack gunfire round about. Sometimes when the guns ranged on one of the more adventurous low flyers they would release their bombs in self defence, and we would hear the crumps round about. This usually meant a turn out and stand-to for fire fighting and rescue parties; however the cool night air was a change from the monotony of the shelters, if not exactly a welcome one. To the west the sky over London reflected the tremendous glow of many fires, and was a witness to those planes that had got through – a sinister reminder of the sufferings of a great city in its agony. Work amongst the shattered remains of houses, with the all pervading acrid smell of damped fire and dust from crumbling brickwork, is a fairly common experience in our country now, but I doubt if it will ever be forgotten by my generation. The rescue of the injured and removal of the dead was tragic enough in all conscience, but it was the smell and dust that seems to stand out in the memory of those nights. The fortitude of the survivors had to be experienced to be believed; they seemed to have been imbued with a strength and faith beyond ordinary mortals and were an inspiration to us all; their homes gone, relations killed or missing, their world in ruins and yet they would be almost jaunty about the whole affair. At times we went out on the day following a raid and cleared debris, blowing down unsafe walls, overhanging roofs and such like jobs in aid of the civil authorities, and helping the victims to recover what possessions were worth saving from the scene of desolation. They would trudge off with handcarts and prams loaded high with the pathetic remains of their homes just glad to be alive and swearing vengeance. Even then, it seemed plain that the enemy would never crush the spirit of the ordinary people. He could destroy their homes but this just kindled a bitter hatred for the Boche.

After a month or two of this strange existence in Kent, 'subject to air attack' as it was so frequently described in the news bulletins, we received orders to move to Northern Ireland to be III Corps Troops Engineers. This was a welcome change, as we all felt it to be the precursor of action once again. We entrained in two troop trains in the small hours of the morning with the usual nightly air raid in progress. Farewells were taken between the formation and their girlfriends in the station yard to the accompaniment of the usual clatter and thumps; perhaps the all pervading darkness was a consolation to the great majority. Perspiring company commanders and section subalterns took a 'poor view' of entraining their men and equipment in inky black-ness without even a glimmer of moonlight. Baggage parties were disturbed by being temporarily separated from their personal weapons. However, it all went off without loss or casualty, the trains pulled out of the station and rumbled slowly through the sleeping countryside by the most circuitous route that the overworked transport department could devise. It was cold weather by now, but the concentration of closely packed human beings quickly steamed up the windows and, except for the odd mouth organ playing, they were soon asleep. After many hours, stops and much shunting, we arrived at Stranraer and with the same process in reverse detrained again in the dark, and embarked for Northern Ireland.

Before we left, the unit had been considerably cheered by a generous number of awards to both officers and men which was in recognition of the stout hearted performance of all ranks in Holland, Belgium and France.

Chapter Twelve

# ULSTER INTERLUDE

We arrived in Larne just before daybreak and it was not long before the unit was speeding westward through lovely countryside. Towards midday we arrived at a little station in County Down and marched four miles to camp, an attractive spot which, as it turned out, was to be our home for over a year. Here we became III Corps Engineers, the whole formation being stationed in Northern Ireland.

Our surroundings consisted of a small river winding round two sides of a hill, with thickly wooded slopes. The hill was surmounted by a castle and by the river bank was a flat strip of terrain just wide enough for the company camps. Nearby was a typical small Irish town, Gildford, near Portadown, with its grey stone houses, market place, and the station of the Royal Ulster Constabulary, watching and waiting for any sign of lawlessness, with rather more earnestness than we associated with a police station in this country. On the outskirts opposite the castle stood a large linen mill; the one local industry. Through the little town ran one wide street with its shops and inns, peopled with the queer mixture of intensely loyal folk and a minority who were not so friendly. Never have troops received a more spontaneous welcome and the months that followed established a firm friendship until, at the day of parting, we might have been the County Down Militia of which they sing over their pots of beer. The inevitable two churches, one Protestant and the other Catholic, showed how religious divisions permeate the lives and thoughts of the people in this delightful land: a fact quite beyond the comprehension of the ordinary Englishman, but there it is, a sort of armed neutrality

102

based upon things of the next world but rigidly applied to the things of this life, without compromise or understanding. Irish hospitality has to be experienced to be appreciated. I suppose it could best be described as benevolent feudalism. While the officers were entertained by the Castle and the managing director of the Mill, the NCOs experienced the thrill of a bit of rabbiting with the surrounding farmers, and every sapper had a 'mother-in-law' for an occasional meal and chat by the fireside in an Irish home.

Meanwhile training, and still more training, resulted in months of practical exercises 'up on wheels'. We got to know the country from Donaghadee to Sion Mills, and Londonderry to Newry, with special references to the rivers! How many times we spent the night bridging those rivers to get divisions over to attack imaginary landings of 'highly mechanized enemy forces which had established a bridgehead at . . .': those treks out to a concentration area before dark, then the dispatch of companies and equipment to forward harbours and concealment until the appropriate moment! If it sounds easy, just ponder the concealment of an RASC bridging train of say sixty vehicles, plus all your own transport from the watchful eye of low flying enemy aircraft and a posse of umpires all eager to justify their existence. The subalterns who went forward on the reconnaissance solemnly swear that they have walked the river banks of all Northern Ireland at one time or another. Meantime I would get their reports back, and after consultation with 'G' staff would allot tasks and equipment, and we would spend yet another night under the stars, manhandling the heavy gear in the silence and murky darkness of a night without a moon. It became a general belief with the men that there was no moonlight in Ireland, a condition noted with considerable emphasis on these occasions.

Sometimes we would lose the 'battle', which meant a withdrawal and this entailed preparing bridges for demolition along a series of river lines. The only real satisfaction obtainable, e.g. blowing up the bridges, was denied us, as apparently the County Council would take a poor view of this and anyway there was no enemy except the umpires, and at times the Directing Staff!

We were still required by the War Office to produce demolition parties on an 'as required' basis and as a result we were allowed the additional manpower to form a Holding Company for this express purpose. It was considered unfair on the Field Companies in the unit who were supporting III Corps to be continually denuded of officers and men.

The Holding Company practised beach landings at a quiet spot on the eastern seaboard that was on Lord Downshire's estate at Dundrum near Newcastle. This entailed hard going, a good quota of duckings and some excitement. A string of craft in tow, loaded with men and equipment in a strong tideway on a dark night can be difficult. At least it calls for a fair degree of watermanship and boat sense, plus a well developed sense of humour. The great compensation for the company was the opportunities offered for netting salmon in the river bounding the estate. With 'local' tuition they became quite expert and any day in season the cook-house bore evidence of the crime. It was surprising how our other Field Companies miles away were anxious to visit them and liaise for not always honourable reasons.

During our stay in Ireland our only contact with the real war, apart from a large party who went to the Middle East and an expedition to Spitzbergen, was on the two occasions when Belfast was raided and we were detailed to assist in clearing up the mess. It was almost like being at home again in South England; all the familiar tasks, the smell and heat of smouldering houses and the demolishing of unsafe structures. Perhaps the highlight was the blowing up of a tapering church spire that was unsafe and leaning. It was one of the few remaining structures we had not tackled at one time or another. There was much professional rivalry about this job within the formation and in the event it was a clean drop without damage to nearby property.

Then there were long marches. As we did not always move about in motor transport, once a week all hands had a route march of about eighteen miles through the surrounding country. The days when this took place were varied, and not announced ahead of time. Out we went, with the band playing a lively air and heads high, after a few miles the hourly halts seemed to get further and further apart, but it is surprising how after a few months training the capacity to stay the distance increased. When approaching camp after these foot slogging exercises, apart from looking red faced and a trifle dusty, with the strident Corps march 'Wings' to stir us on, we threw out our chests, and told each other that we could have gone for another twenty miles. This hardening process was varied with cross country work and night marches, but perhaps the highlight was a periodical trek of sixty or seventy miles to a distant range; this used to take three days each way, bivouacking at night under the trees and enjoying every minute. Strangely enough the scores on the ranges were better too, than on occasions when for want of time we went in vehicles.

Short of being at war, this enforced period of waiting in Ireland was excellent value as regards training, and a pleasant experience which left its mark upon the formation; even the band adopted one or two Irish airs as part of its repertoire. Some of the more adventurous of the Corps married colleens to show their faith in the country. The highlight was a very occasional weekend in plain clothes down in Dublin, where the lighted shops and crowded streets gave one a reminder of pre-war conditions. One could buy a box of chocolates or silk stockings in anticipation of the next seven days leave in England, see a good show at the Abbey Theatre, visit the Curragh for an afternoon at the races, or merely sit in the lounge of the Gresham Hotel for a while, and watch the world and his wife go by. It is surprising what can be squeezed into forty-eight hours. The streets were fairly full of the soldiers of Eire, well turned out in the main, although mostly very young and rather shorter than our men. An occasional priest and members of a religious order jostling with the crowd of shoppers in O'Connell Street gave the place an odd air of neutrality; it seemed as though they were almost expecting war to come to them, but hoping that it would not. So many appeared to be sympathetic to the cause of the Allied nations that it was not easy to understand the peculiar position their government had maintained. Perhaps the most incongruous sight was the German and Italian flags in front of their consulates; a strange land indeed!

Perhaps the most widely appreciated amusements of the troops were the dances held in Lurgan Assembly rooms; these occasions were literally a manifestation of 'Finnegan's Ball' itself come to life, where sapper, gunner and infanteer swung round with the local youth and beauty to the strains of a caley band. Many of the lads walked home anything up to twenty miles after the show rather than miss the fun, which is more surprising when one considers the tempo of the dances. The whole affair was a breath-taking gallop from start to finish, with stout and porter thrown in to help things along. It is no wonder that in addition to a few broken hearts, some heads suffered the same fate.

During the intervals in training and when we were not employed on 'works', that mystic word which covers anything from erecting temporary huts to permanent construction of one type or another, we were collecting engineer intelligence on roads, rivers, bridges, fords and, in general, the local resources of the six counties. This took us through the countryside from the hills in the west to the seaboard on the east, and brought us in contact with the country folk in the countless villages and hamlets. What a fund of amusement they were to us. No doubt they thought the same of us, particularly when the troops were detailed to assist in the unwelcome task of flax gathering.

If you open the Old Testament and turn to Nehemiah, look up the fourth chapter and run your finger down to the seventeenth verse you will read the following:

> *They which builded on the wall, and they that have burdens, with those that laded, <u>every one</u> with one of his hands wrought in the work, and with the other <u>hand</u> held a weapon. For the builders, every one had his sword girded by his side, and <u>so</u> builded.*

Now it seems fairly obvious that Nehemiah must have been the first sapper. Not for one minute do I suppose they called him Director of Works, or Engineer in Chief in those days, but the simple fact stands out a mile. He had the idea which has been handed down through the centuries to the present day sapper; he was probably the first military bricklayer. The simplicity and clarity of the specifications shame the modern Army Council instruction by its directness. Taking Nehemiah's precept as a guide, it is easy to see why we must build as well as fight. We have erected literally thousands of tin igloos styled Nissen huts, at the same time defacing many a decent property that remains in our fair land. Who has not entered a stately park, surrounded by a baronial wall, with its shady trees and elegant sweeps of parkland about some ancient home only to emerge some weeks later having transformed the whole place into serried rows of those tin-tack tabernacles! But there, the modern army must live somewhere. As if not content with our handiwork, we have driven roads hither and thither, put up incinerators, cookhouses and all the other eyesores scheduled as camp structures.

One can almost hear the modern Nehemiah saying as he enters a certain high building in Whitehall, 'What about these sappers – are they holding their weapons at the correct angle?' Calling his staff together to write instructions, training manuals, pocket books weighing many pounds and textbooks, all to teach the sapper how to hold and use that weapon in his other hand. (I wonder if the great Creator really feels that he gave the sapper one hand too few?) This elaboration of Nehemiah's simple specification is forwarded 'for information and necessary action' through the appropriate channels, as it goes out in ever widening circles. Probably the medical branch is consulted for confirmation that sappers still have one spare hand; in any case the result is the same. Our sapper holds, wields, carries or has strapped to him various weapons and all the other warlike appliances of any infantry soldier. An interesting sidelight is that the instructions, training manuals, pocket books and pamphlets are all at great pains to point out that the building, lading, modern slaves of Nehemiah are COMBATANT TROOPS. Personally we could never think the individual sapper was in any danger of over-looking this aspect of his calling, judging from his appearance when dressed in battle order and close to the enemy.

When the troops have exhausted their patience roofing huts with tin sheets which harass and cut the hands, they break into brickwork and carry on the good work of 'those who laded' as the first Director of Works specified. At times when all the troops on hand are housed, they turn their attention to the RAF and lash out in concrete by the way of an extra aerodrome or two. Here the sappers really get down to it, with the aid of every modern mechanical appliance, literally plastering the fair face of the countryside with miles and miles of concrete runways. As if to prevent ideas becoming stereotyped the Herrenvolk come over

107

and mutilate some town and indeed biblical prophecy brings the Corps into its own. They follow up those good Christian souls who minister to the suffering and once they have got the remains of the town in their hands, then you see some lading. They pull down, blow up and drag things away until an unappreciative borough surveyor thinks that the sappers have done more harm than the Germans.

But enough of this building and lading; take another look at the specifications, not only must we be 'in the work' but, leaving nothing to chance, we must hold a weapon in the other hand. This is clearly the mandate. When the entire 'weapon holding' really gets down to the ordinary soldiers, styled Field Companies RE, then things begin to happen. They take us out for days at a time waging a bloody war against Redland or Blueland. We go forward, carry out the necessary reconnaissance for assault over rivers (crossing by the perfectly good existing bridge if no umpire is about). At night we build girder bridges, or in an incredibly short time float pontoon equipment across the gap. I am not sure whether sappers regard humping pontoon units over a ploughed field in the dark as 'LADING' or as 'WEAPON HOLDING'. Most of the muttered words and expression of opinion that I have heard on these occasions did not sound like either and are not repeatable.

When the season for formation (all arms) training is temporarily over – for like pheasant shooting it has a season – and when the shortage of huts, bricks and cement is acute, they take us to the ranges where flattening our tummies on the ground we really get down to the weapon holding business. If it is a fine day, without too much wind and shooting is in danger of becoming enjoyable, the formation gas officer comes upon the scene and gets us into gas masks. When the order comes round that no further ammunition will be issued until the next training period, what does a CRE do then? He makes them dig cunning holes in the ground and wrap the place round with skilfully concealed barbed wire.

At the end of the day when all are back in camp, the education officer gives a lecture on the 'modern army', the padre holds a prayer meeting, cadre classes for budding lance corporals begin, study groups sit down to work and a company sing song strikes up in the NAAFI. Meanwhile the section officers sit down to censor the men's letters and then there are the visits and inspections by the staff.

On one occasion a general appeared at one of our camps; everything according to specification, gold oak leaves, red hatband and gorgets, brassard on arm, three rows of decorations, highly polished Sam Browne and field boots that dazzled. The guard turned out, were duly inspected in every detail and then dismissed. Meanwhile a well brought-up sapper dashed into the company office and 'spilled the beans' that something was happening at the Quarter Guard!

Now it so happened that on this particular afternoon the Company Commander was out, on official business be it noted, likewise the second in command. A hasty beat round by the CSM produced a newly joined subaltern whom he sat down in the OC's chair. To lend colour to appearances in his strange surroundings, he began making notes from the latest training manual in the pending tray in front of him.

In due course the great one entered and faced the young man. 'I am General Snodgrass' quoted the visitor by way of introduction. By this time all attempts at realism, or even clear thinking was quite beyond the unhappy lad who promptly sprang to attention and saluted oblivious of the fact that he was bareheaded. The General sat down. The impressed representative of the OC mumbled the necessary apologies and explanations for the absence of his Company Commander. By this time the General, who turned out to be a very senior welfare officer, made his mission known. This was sufficiently encouraging to prompt the young officer to suggest the unit needed wireless sets as they only had one. The reply was, 'We have none on hand – but I will make a note of it. Good afternoon.'

Curtains.

Then, of course, we all shared in another kind of occupation, which is something between running a hotel, life as a Justices' Clerk in a petty sessions and an accountant. This is styled 'Administration'. It would be unwise to say much about the threadbare subject of 'filling in forms', that persistent blight that

109

intrudes upon our existence from the cradle to the grave. Precious little can be done in any phase of life nowadays without having to fill in a form to say when you were born, where you live, what you earn and those left behind when you die. In the Army they manage this form filling bee on intensive lines, even to the extent of running schools to teach the form filling habit to young aspirants for high positions. The matter does not stop there, however, for these 'form conscious' young men, when they become sufficiently senior discover that with the aid of the duplicator they can invent new forms, styled pro forma to distinguish the issue from the printed variety. With increasing experience these improvisations can be made even more difficult than the official forms. Then they send them out to a perspiring soldiery. Experience in the formation headquarters went to show that it is necessary to fill in 2.5 forms every day, seven days a week, e.g. over 900 per annum. If the requisite numbers of copies are used as a multiplier, the latter figure reaches over 3,000 sheets of paper containing statistical information.

Still another diversion for the young officers are Courts of Enquiry. These are convened by order of the CO. Three or four officers assemble at a time and place arranged, on a date specified, to examine witnesses and ascertain what happened to the missing blanket etc. In certain circumstances the Courts apportion blame, then when the proceedings (in quadruplicate) go back to the convenor, Sapper Smith usually has to pay or at least make some contribution to the National Exchequer according to his degree of delinquency. These proceedings are recorded upon a special Army Form, signed by all members of the board, each witnessed and then the forms are finally endorsed by the CO stamped with the office stamp and the party is over. Of course Higher Command may disagree with the endorsements, the method adopted by the Court, any or all of the evidence and then back comes the transcript again for the next session. During our stay in Ireland while quarrying one day a lone goat dropped dead nearby, well away from the blasting be it noted. Now the nanny was in an interesting condition and an asset to its owner who claimed the value of the goat and expected kid from the CO of the Field Company on this job. The result was a Court of Enquiry to ascertain the cause of the death of a pregnant goat on the date specified. These proceedings became a classic and circulated sub rosa quite a way to cause many a laugh.

Then there is the 'concert'. Amongst the troops this function is taken really seriously. It represents the high spot of the co-operative ability, initiative, power to improvise and organization within the unit. Usually led by one of the subalterns and backed up by the sergeants, the performers steal off to some unoccupied shed or hut to rehearse. A fine display of minor tactics begins to be used in the life and the work of the company to account for people missing from ordinary parades and duties. The whole atmosphere is permeated with excuses for absences. Things in the company do not seem to be running quite as smoothly as usual; all sorts of people are missing at awkward times. Much depends upon the outlook of the OC at this critical stage; generally speaking it is considered strategically sound to keep him in the dark for as long as possible.

One day, towards the time of presentation of the performance, while on his rounds of the camp accompanied by the CSM, the OC may see the odd figure of a large raw-boned soldier, clad only in the scantiest female attire with a blonde wig, emerge from a hut. Recovering from his first shock, he is reassured that the morals of the company are as good as ever and it is merely the men rehearsing. After this stage the prospective concert assumes, quite unjustifiably, an official role and carpenters and electricians, scenic artists, musicians and whole cross sections of the unit become involved in the production of the show. Eventually the great night arrives and the whole unit squeezes into the impro-vised hall, where officers and men, packed in serried rows, are determined to enjoy themselves – and they do. The audience is quite prepared to take a hand in the proceedings if the fare provided does not come up to expectations. Much good humoured barracking and chaff is exchanged and, generally speaking, no quarter is either given or expected between performers and those on the other side of the footlights.

All the usual items of song and dance go with a swing, in any company there are always a few men with real musical ability, and every item is enjoyed either because it is good, or on account of

111

the fun its poor quality provides the audience. The high spot of the evening is usually the sketch, in which the parts of company officers are played by the men in some such setting as the orderly room or at a kit inspection. All kinds of ridiculous situations are produced in quick succession to give the players an opportunity to imitate mannerisms or favourite expressions used by their officers. This invariably brings the house down and rounds off a rollicking night. These shows got up by the men themselves invariably please far more than the entertainment provided by outside agencies. One finds too that the unit that is good at its job is the unit which usually produces the best shows which I suppose is an indication of their cooperative ability and team spirit.

Hence it comes about that those humble disciples of Nehemiah, when not actually demolishing the works of others, building and lading themselves, or putting all else aside and indulging in an orgy of form filling, entertain each other and keep happy. One thing is certain, there is plenty on hand to keep them from becoming bored.

Another feature of life is best summoned up in the letters MT, for the mechanical transport of a formation brings great responsibility for training, maintenance and exercise, even in the peaceful surroundings of life at home. The raw material drafted in as drivers, RE, is a perpetual headache to most Company Commanders. They are lectured about the mysteries of the internal combustion engine, how it 'comes in here and goes out there', the intricacies of gearbox and differential, together with all the other odds and ends of a modern vehicle. They are then introduced to the art of map reading by an NCO who explains the necessity for three distinct types of North, magnetic, grid and true, after which they are put in the lorries for further practical instruction. Then the fun begins in deadly earnest. After spells in hospital and attendances at inquests, the survivors eventually emerge to be rediscovered as impeccable drivers in some night convoy. But it all takes time and patience, quite a lot of work for the workshops, an odd job or two for the doctors and plenty of form filling for the second in command.

The more adventurous are trained as dispatch riders, that peculiar breed of young men who seem to have missed their vocation by not joining the RAF. We had one with us in Ireland who, when he saw cattle ahead of the convoy, would zoom off at high speed, stop just short of the rear animal and put his engine into a succession of ear splitting backfires. The cows jumped over the hedges and with the road clear, the convoy would go through and this otherwise law abiding lad would meekly rejoin his section formation.

Such was our daily round, much the same as any other Field Company of the Royal Engineers, and as far as our domestic life goes, the same as any unit of the British Army.

Then came the time when rather more than usual activity at a certain port, all of which was mysterious at the time, was followed by the arrival of the Americans. They quickly infiltrated the whole country and soon our men were rubbing shoulders with the jaunty young men from 'over there'. They too were well received by the Northern Counties, but the press in Eire reacted rather violently just in case they ventured south of the border.

The months slipped by, and with many postings away on promotion to other units, in addition to a contingent that went to the Middle East, and one or two jobs, it almost seemed as if we were in Ireland for the remainder of the war. Having commanded the unit since 1932 when it was raised, and in our many vicissitudes during wartime, I left the unit on promotion. A leave taking that was, to be sure! Before moving on, one of my last acts as CO was to find a niche for Corporal Holland who had been my driver and batman since the outset of war. He had taken on considerably more responsibilities in the running and administration in the HQ in the last year or so. The Holding Company, who were just leaving us and converting into a parachute squadron, needed an MT sergeant. I had no reservations about sending him down to them and he was delighted. He was a very high grade man and popular in the unit so they had no doubts about accepting him.

Chapter Thirteen

# SPITZBERGEN

For some months, while the main body were in Ireland, a detachment had been maintained at the Naval Barracks at Devonport to carry out operations in Spain should Hitler decide to strike south from France. But as our jobs were often secret this did not cause much comment. This detachment consisted of Major Sammy Green, four officers and 100 NCOs and men of 297 Field Park Company who had joined us in Gravesend. During these months a large amount of training in addition to the usual arts and crafts associated with sappers, was put in on watermanship, sailing and general boat drill which produced an atmosphere of mystery. The time slipped by pleasantly except for one tragic occasion when an air raid robbed us of twenty-five of our men by a direct hit upon a shelter. All hands of the contingent became more and more naval in their outlook. They had reached the stage when they talked of going aboard and going ashore when entering or leaving their camp.

On a sun splashed summer Sunday in 1941, a church parade was in progress and the unit was all present, polished and scrubbed, and equipment freshly dabbed with khaki blanco No. 3. They sat squeezed together in the pews listening to the sermon. The service was nearly over, the familiar psalms and hymns had been sung and the preacher had got to the stage when one could detect almost subconsciously by tone and pitch of voice rather than logic that he was running dry. The heat of the day, the peaceful surroundings and maybe the sermon, had produced a mental serenity among the troops which the sergeant major described as going to sleep, only more forcefully! Into this quiet atmosphere the staccato clatter of a pair of army boots up the aisle caused all to rouse themselves and restart mind and imagination. It was 'waiting duties' from the guard so they thought this must be urgent as they watched him hand Sammy Green an envelope. For some this was the beginning of a journey to the far north.

After they marched back from the church to the parade ground, before being dismissed, an order was issued by Major Green for three officers and thirty men to re-muster in battle order with their kit in an hour's time and be ready to move. As our units had served under the command of the British Army, the French Army, and frequently under Naval Command, it did not surprise them greatly when the party was ordered to report for operations under command of a Canadian force which was assembling in the vicinity.

After an address by the rear admiral of the dockyard, this contingent under Green left the naval depot to the strains of our regimental march played by a Royal Marine Band, and entrained for an unknown destination. After the usual long train journey and the inevitable transit camp – how the men swear about this feature of army life – they found themselves aboard a large British troopship with several hundred Canadians including Major Walsh of the Royal Canadian Engineers with his 3 Canadian Field Company. He was acting CRE of the force. Almost as soon as they were aboard they weighed anchor and slipped silently away from the port.

During the outward voyage there was a good deal to keep them occupied with practice drills for surface raider attack, boat stations, dummy air raid alarms, abandoning ship and so forth. Their off duty time was devoted to fraternizing with the Canadians.

One stirring event on the outward voyage, which greatly impressed all ranks, was a chance meeting with a large Atlantic convoy en route for Great Britain. Coming up over the horizon with their escort vessels, they steamed majestically past, an apt illustration of how the life of our nation depends upon sea power.

So far the average speed of the expedition was about 18 knots until, arriving off Iceland, they dropped anchor for a few hours. Here they met American naval officers who came out and visited the ships and enjoyed British hospitality. As a matter of fact one young American officer enjoyed himself so much that he forgot to disembark and it was only after an exchange of signals and the holding up of the whole convoy that he was eventually returned to his own dry ship!

As the troopship was strongly protected by an escort of HM ships, it was freely conjectured that it was to be another 'party'. Speculation was rife throughout the ship's company as to their destination; bets were offered and taken. One enterprising Canadian was running a regular book in which you could take your choice from the Arctic to the Antarctic. After a lapse of several days, steaming north with the weather getting colder and colder, there was very little left to guess about. The whole affair was just strange. The mystery was increased by the arrival of still more naval units who joined the escort.

When well out to sea and nearing the objective, the Canadian Commander held a conference with the senior officers, and outlined the plan. This in turn was put to the men, section by section, and procedure was discussed in every detail. Variations had to be arranged according to the circumstances on arrival as it was not known whether or not the landing would be opposed.

At this stage all ranks were given thick woollen underclothing, socks, ski-boots, leather jerkins and sheepskin coats. Having donned these outfits they looked and felt really tough! As the convoy neared Spitzbergen, which they now knew was the expedition's destination, the men who had also been provided with life jackets and caps, slept fully dressed with their small arms readily accessible.

On the fifth day out they were in the Arctic Circle. The brilliant sunshine of the first few days gave way to cold foggy weather and the extra warmth of their special clothing was appreciated as also was the ration issue of rum. The next day was very cold with a clear blue sky and a smooth sea. Meanwhile the ships kept up their steady progress. In an effort to keep out the cold, frequent PT was now the main feature of activities.

The seventh day brought further cold and foggy weather, with

116

the expedition still steaming north. During the day, final arrangements for disembarkation were completed and Russian and Norwegian interpreters were attached to all parties, all secret instructions destroyed and final operation orders given to Group Commanders. Speed was reduced to 8 knots and they dropped anchor in one of the fjords the same evening. A large school of whales in the vicinity proved to be the main item of interest – an entirely new experience for most of the ships' company.

An idea of the background may be gained from the following brief description of this strange northern land. It is light for the whole of the twenty-four hours in the summer and this perhaps is the most unusual feature. At home one punctuates one's existence by day and night but out there you wake up at midnight, look at your watch which says twelve o'clock. You look out of the porthole to find it is broad daylight and that leaves one in the uncomfortable position of not knowing whether it is midnight or high noon. The island of Spitzbergen, or more correctly the Spitzbergen Archipelago is between 10 degrees and 35 degrees E. longitude and 74 degrees and 81 degrees N. latitude. The biggest island is almost the size of England and Scotland, with two others to the east and west respectively, each about the size of Ireland; these are separated from the central mainland by channels. The first view reveals a barren mountainous region, utterly devoid of vegetation of any kind, snow-capped hills and numerous deep navigable fjords running inland. Glaciers reflect the light even more brilliantly than the snow covered wastes. The sea is bright and broken by ice floes, and at places, is frozen over and merges with the land. The air is crisp and clear with a blue sky in which birds wheel and skim the surface of the sea and land. Everywhere divers, gulls, puffins, geese and eider ducks abound.

Ashore seams of coal can be seen running horizontally and also outcrops on the sides of the hills, hence the mining settlements of Norwegians and Russians. These communities live in separate towns and do not appear to mix to any extent. The seasonal presence of whales in these waters brings the whaling fleets and the whale oil industry onto the island; the only other occupation, save for a few trappers working inland. These trappers were later brought in to the coastal towns by messages dropped by an aeroplane and they turned up loaded with pelts. Blue fox, white fox, polar bear and reindeer being their quarry. These beautiful skins represent in themselves a great story of hardihood, courage and adventure, before they reach their market as luxury clothing to adorn the women of many lands; many months of dark skies, gales and blizzards weed out all but the strongest of men and beast alike.

The day of arrival, the ship anchored in deep water off the Russian settlement of Barentsburg; from here the outcrop of coal on the mountainside was easily visible. The ninth day saw the disembarkation and landing of the troops, who, right from the first, were received in the friendliest manner by the inhabitants. The commander of the force met the civilian officials, and made arrangements for the complete evacuation of the entire population of the island. Our party was given its objectives, and split up accordingly, one section going to the Russian settlement of Grumantly and the others to Pyramiden about four hours steaming from there.

Going ashore in naval pinnaces, the party was met by the Russians who seemed overjoyed and expressed their feelings by clapping hands. They gave the troops cigarettes and chocolates, with which they seemed to be better supplied than most NAAFI canteens at home. Meanwhile stores were unloaded, and after a brief reconnaissance, tasks allocated. All demolition here was completed in eight hours, after which the sappers, with their new found friends the Russians, embarked in HM ship and took passage to Barentsburg arriving at four o'clock the following morning.

The sappers then went to their next port of call, Ny Alesund, where further work of demolition and scorched earth had by now become a matter of daily routine. Our second party had worked continuously for twenty-four hours, destroying the mines and coal stocks at Grumantly and they then re-embarked for food and sleep. The first party went to Barentsburg to assist in the general evacuation of the place prior to certain final demolitions.

The sight of those vast coal stocks, burning furiously against the high background of the snow capped mountains and glaciers as they withdrew, was truly remarkable. Just picture thousands of tons of coal on fire in that Arctic setting . . .

The eleventh day they arrived back at Barentsburg and met those who had been to Ny Alesund and Sveagruva. But life is more than houses and machinery, there were live stock, horses, cows, pigs and domestic animals which could not be just abandoned and had to be slaughtered. The sappers thought that this was perhaps the toughest job of the lot. The depressing sight of this deserted town with the slaughtered animals lying there, for these had been shot, was an unpleasant memory although they were able to enjoy a meal from a huge beast which was roasted in the embers.

The evacuation of the inhabitants was very thoroughly organized, even to the extent of planes flying inland over miles of barren and desolate snow covered wastes, to warn trappers to return to town.

The work of demolition was systematically carried on at Ny Alesund and the Norwegian settlements of Longyearby and Sveagruva, Pyramiden, Grumantly and Barentsburg. All fuel stocks were fired; possibly a quarter of a million tons. Mining machinery and similar equipment was blown up, and rendered useless. Large stocks of mine explosives were destroyed; in one case as much as eight tons.

Before the large dumps of coal could be ignited it was necessary to cut adits or galleries leading into the pits, so as to ensure an adequate supply of air for combustion. As these huge heaps were above ground and frozen, this job was rather like working inside a refrigerator. It was literally like cutting one's way through a conglomeration of coal and solid ice. The labour involved was considerable, and although the operation turned out to be unopposed, the task was an arduous undertaking for the troops, as the weather was at times severe and at the very best, cold. At night, at some of the anchorages, the sea froze and ice floes were a fairly common sight. Amongst the new experiences, at least to our men, in this strange and barren land, was the sight of arctic seals, polar bears, reindeer and arctic fox at Sveagruva.

Towards the end of this brief occupation, an incident occurred

119

which might well have proved disastrous. In the early hours of the morning, the wooden town of Barentsburg caught fire. Troops were sleeping in some of the houses and turned out to fight the flames. For a while it looked as if the flames had been isolated, but eventually they spread and the whole place was burned to the ground.

Towards the end all equipment and stores, including as much as possible of the belongings of the Norwegians and Russians, were ferried out and put aboard the troopship; no small task in itself. The trappers refused to be parted from their dogs, nor was it conceivably possible to destroy them, so they were evacuated with their fellow human beings. They came aboard like well disciplined troops, their masters directing them with a few laconic commands of 'right, left, stop' and so forth. This caused great amusement amongst the troops who all agreed that there must be a training battalion somewhere for huskies.

The last scene in the drama was the final departure from Longyearby, which was carried out with traditional ceremony; the Norwegian flag was hauled down and the last post was sounded. Whereas for some days past the hills had shuddered with the reverberations of demolitions, now the ghostly echoes of those final notes came back from the hills as if to indicate a happier future in the days to come.

Eventually at eleven o'clock in the evening on the eighteenth day from home, the expedition weighed anchor and headed southwards. About 200 Free French officers accompanied the party on their homeward voyage. They had escaped from concentration camps in Poland and crossed the frontier into Russia. They were overjoyed at the prospect of rejoining their compatriots; several spoke English and told tales of cruelty and hardship at the hands of the Hun and then talked of the people who write to our papers at home about the 'poor Germans' as if to distinguish them from the Nazis. One of these Frenchmen told a crazy story of how he got into Russia disguised as a peasant by driving a herd of cattle over the border before Russia had entered the war. So great was the Russian sense of neutrality that they interned him but politely returned the cattle to the Germans.

During the voyage home the weather was fine, the sea calm and

120

with the increasing warmth spirits rose until, at 11 p.m. on the twenty-second day, the anchor was dropped in a home port. The job is perhaps best summed up by the chance remark of a Canadian, overheard just before disembarking; 'Funny job this dropping salt on the tails of the Herrenvolk'.

## Chapter Fourteen

# GIBRALTAR

It was while in Ireland that an order was passed through our HQ fixing the time and place for me to meet the GOC.-in-C. Gibraltar, in London. Within forty-eight hours a small party left for an unknown destination on a mission. They were commanded by Paul Baker, recently promoted to major, with three subalterns, Lieutenants Roy Meyler, Don Terry, and 'Shorty' Wells and five good NCOs who were drawn from across the Field Companies under protest from their OCs ! The nature of the mission that could not be revealed to the men until they left England, was to advise and train the garrison of Gibraltar in the techniques of destroying bulk fuel installations.

The party travelled to Gourock and was embarked on HMS *Maidstone*, a submarine depot ship due to take up station on the Rock. Baker's description of the departure was as follows:

> *Before we left Gourock a team of officers was sent out to scour the town to buy ginger ale for the Wardroom bar to mix with brandy in 'horses' necks', which were very popular. The odd thing was that the ginger ale cost more in the Wardroom than the duty free brandy! When we sailed we joined a convoy and for a time as we passed through the North Atlantic one of our escorts was the mighty battleship* King George V, *known as KG five. I remember thinking as she followed us that her beam looked like a destroyer crossing our course at right angles.*

Soon after embarking the party was impressed into the ship's crew. All had previously experienced more than one passage with the Royal Navy and could avoid the more obvious pitfalls set for the unsuspecting soldier aboard ship but this was different. They not only had to avoid any reference to the sharp or blunt end, they had to be sailors; it was not sufficient merely to be careful to refer to ladders or companionways as such, and not as stairs.

Baker played around with division lists, quarter bills, action stations for military personnel and generally became entered as apprentice to 'Jimmy-the-One'. Furthermore, they helped man the ack-ack guns and kept anti-submarine lookouts throughout the voyage so this time they felt part of the ship and not on the ship as landlubbers as they were usually described.

'Jimmy-the-One' was also the gunnery officer and would frequently exercise gun teams. Now sappers are sappers and gunners are gunners, that is in the army, but this did not mean a thing to the naval officers. At first our party meekly suggested that it 'warn't their trade' but this was brushed aside. Then they threw themselves heart and soul into the job because they couldn't let the army down. Before the end of the voyage they achieved the impossible and those sappers were gunners, hopping round at their stations and obeying orders for change of targets like any matelot wearing a gun on his sleeve. As one NCO put it 'Aint it all right, chum, you have to do everything in the navy, gunner and all'.

Many alarms relieved these watches of any tendency to boredom. Every distant gull seemed like a plane in sight and the humble porpoise invariably appeared like a submarine to the unaccustomed eye.

Every morning at dawn the Tannoys would summon the watch to action stations, where they were compensated by witnessing the splendour of the rising sun over the Atlantic Ocean. Sometimes calm and comparatively cloudless, but at others it would appear angry and tempestuous as the light spread across the watery expanse. In either case it gave one a sense of proportion, and man's efforts dwarfed into insignificance against this background of sea and sky with the rising of the sun. But the reverie was soon ended for there was much to be done each day.

The spells off duty were spent either on a hand of cards or swapping yarns, whilst the NCOs tried out the possibility of investing the 'old mud hook' at Crown and Anchor, only to find that if it provided excitement, it was not too good a pastime from the financial point of view. The Royal Navy are great hosts and the time passed pleasantly enough. At one period they ran into heavy weather, when the troops were rather shaken, particularly at breakfast time when heavy rolling landed them either in the scuppers or under the mess tables with their breakfast wrapped round their necks. The routine during the voyage was a change for the party who quickly fell in with the traditions of life afloat; after all, they had worked under Naval Command in many of their 'jobs' and the White Ensign figured in most of their recollections. They came up smiling for meals, in spite of the weather and learned to sleep in a hammock. An amusing indication of our close association with the sea for some months is that many in the unit had got into the habit of 'making signals' in preference to sending messages; this produced an inquiry while on an exercise in Ireland from a brigadier who asked whether we were 'blankety, blank' Marines!

The days at sea passed quickly and one morning the Spanish and African coasts came into view. These blue hills, misty and distant, merging at places with the sea and sky, told of the end of the journey. It was not long before that huge bluff, the rock itself, was discernible, dominating and impressive, standing sentinel over the entrance to what the chief *dago* was wont to refer to as *mare nostrum*. I know of no spectacle more impressive or more typical of our solidarity as an Empire than the first glimpse of Gibraltar as one approaches from the sea. The key position of the Rock at the western end of the Mediterranean is at once evident when approaching from the Atlantic. The massive block of grey rock rising steeply to 1,400 feet in grim and imposing outline gives a vivid idea of the military importance of the place. The north and east faces are particularly steep, but elsewhere the sides descend in terraces to sea level.

Baker continued:

*We had a comfortable trip and duly took up quarters on arrival. I then reported to the Garrison HQ and explained our mission. Practically all the sappers on the Rock were tunnellers, mostly former miners, and a tough lot. The rest of my party were intro-*

124

*duced to them and got on with a programme of training in demolitions under Don Terry, boatmanship under Roy Meyler with Wells and the NCOs helping out as needed. As a change from tunnelling they found this most acceptable and we heard that there had eventually been some keen competition to get into one of our raiding parties.*

The amazing collection of barracks, casemates of bygone ages, modern fortifications, a Moorish castle, and countless other works of the military engineer, tended to give the place an intriguing outline. It may be said that the Corps of Royal Engineers had its origin at Gibraltar in the late eighteenth century as soldier artificers.

The outstanding impression of those first contacts with the garrison was that everyone tried to convince them that there was no escape from the Rock for the duration. Once you set a foot ashore, you were there for keeps, seemed to be the local outlook and any suggestion that one might return to England was the subject of merriment and derision.

The naval base and dockyards bring the two services close together at this outpost of the Empire. It will be recalled that Gibraltar was taken by the British in 1704 and has been a colony of the Crown ever since; small wonder then with its dominating position and historical importance if the Nazis should cast covetous eyes on it. The indigenous population are descendants of Italian, Spanish or early Genoese settlers, but of course are British now and highly patriotic subjects of His Majesty. Local legend says that British rule will last as long as the monkeys flourish. This refers to the small colony of Barbary apes found on the Rock who are officially on the 'ration strength' of the garrison and a bombardier has a full time job as their minder.

The party was accommodated in Nissen huts up near the frontier on the isthmus. Little or no blackout was in force – that was a minor thrill. It was quite exciting to see the lights again at night, their only previous similar experience since war was at Nantes just before the fall of France, and those more recent weekends in Dublin.

The work of the mission was hard, at first often taking up long hours, but once accomplished it became a matter of waiting for the passage home, not too easy a matter in those days. During this period of waiting several of the officers and NCOs did spells at sea with the anti-submarine patrol. Imagine leaving the trawler base, 'pens' as they are known, and pushing out to sea early on a wet and cold morning, as likely as not into the teeth of a Levanter. Life aboard these hard little ships is tough going at the best and hell at other times. With a small crew commanded by a lieutenant, they go out to hunt, fight and destroy the King's enemies above and below the sea. On these spells at sea our men would muster and carry on as part of the crew. They learned the secrets of the Asdic by which they listened to the grating of the surf miles away inshore, or the thump, thump of some distant coaster's screw plugging along on her lawful business. They would keep watch either above or below deck in the engine room and generally share the rough and the smooth with those cheery young men in these ships. One of our NCOs went to the lengths of re-plumbing the hot and cold water pipes to the galley with such crowning success that both the hot and the cold water came out of their appropriately labelled taps when the job was done! Action stations and alarms came frequently enough to convince the most bloodthirsty that there was plenty of excitement to be had in these small but active vessels of the Royal Navy.

The Rock, because of its size, only had a limited garrison, a fair proportion of which were RE tunnelling companies including one RCE from Canada. These were engaged in hollowing out even more of the interior of the Rock to provide shelter for the garrison in the event of air attack. In the end total living space was provided including a hospital and all the necessary facilities for a long stay. New gun emplacements were constructed covering the isthmus joining the Rock to Spain. The spoil from all the recent work was tipped into the sea adjoining the narrow neck of land connecting the Rock to Spain and this was used to form a landing and take-off strip for fighter aircraft; as the tunnelling progressed so the airstrip runway was extended.

The weekly ceremony of the Keys was a never failing source of interest. The battalions of the garrison took it in turn to provide the band and escort to the Keys; the Independent Company provided a frontier guard. After inspection by the governor or another officer appointed by him, the frontier guard marched through the casemates to their posts, and the gates were then closed and 'locked' by the Keys sergeant. The arrival of the sergeant at the gate is always challenged by the sentry, and the traditional dialogue is then,

'Who goes there'?

'Keys.'

'Whose Keys'?

'King George's Keys.'

Rumour has it that on one occasion before the sergeant could reply to the latter question, a wit in the crowd convulsed his fellow onlookers by interjecting loudly 'Maconochies'! It should be remembered that in wartime the garrison menu comes very largely out of tins bearing that trade name and so is well known to all ordinary soldiers of two major wars.

Sergeant Blake, who was awarded a Military Medal at Rotterdam, was walking down a street one day when the Commander-in-Chief, Field Marshal Lord Gort VC, was approaching. Blake chucked him up a smart salute, as the soldiers would say, and the Field Marshal spotted his MM. He stopped and had quite a long conversation with him. Later, during an inspection on one parade in which the sapper officers and NCOs were fallen in as supernumeraries at the back, the Governor, Lord Gort, spotted Sergeant Blake again and going up to him said, 'I know you'. He then carried on with their previous conversation. It took Sergeant Blake a long time to live down his acquaintance with a Field Marshal in the Sergeants' Mess.

Baker signalled the War Office to report the completion of their work and request permission to rejoin their unit in Northern Ireland. After a week or two of waiting and considerable negotiations, prompted no doubt by a homing instinct acquired during previous adventures on the Dutch and French seaboard, the party received the order for embarkation. This was a great day, for in spite of the many friends and enjoyable experiences, a man without a definite job is a poor creature. So it was that at last they said goodbye having disproved the wartime adage 'once at Gib – always at Gib', and sailed in a small steamer in company with other details. As fellow passengers there were British officers who had escaped from the Hun in France and made their way back through Spain. They told tales of Spanish prisons, vermin, starvation, Gestapo, misery and suffering; also of many months of hard living after the escape before their delivery was accomplished.

Finally our men arrived back in their unit lines four months after leaving, with a tan the colour of mahogany and no funds in credit, only to face a barrage of chaff about their 'tough' mission away from wartime Britain.

## Chapter Fifteen

# GREECE

It was during the time that we were still in England that Major Bert West and I left for a few days. That the officer concerned commanded the company next in turn for a 'job', did not escape the notice of the others, and as may be imagined, our departure was generally accepted to portend that something was in the air. By this time the prelude to these parties was beginning to be understood and accepted as part of the ordinary life of the unit. What was expressed by knowing glances exchanged in the Officers' Mess and, maybe a wink and a nod in the Sergeants' Mess, found more concrete expression when a sapper would let up on his task and confide to his work mates that 'another job was coming off soon'.

Hence it came about that shortly after our return on a cold winter's day towards the end of 1940, West and six officers with a fairly large contingent left their training ground under orders for a certain port of embarkation. West had sealed orders, which would only be opened on arrival at their destination, prior to reporting ashore to a certain senior officer. Accordingly they boarded one of HM troopships with certain familiar war-like stores and equipment, without any idea that they were to take part in the last act of what has now come to be regarded as an epic struggle against overwhelming odds.

The troopship left dock at midday, moving out into the stream until the late afternoon, when she weighed anchor and put to sea in convoy with two other vessels, escorting destroyers, cruisers, an aircraft carrier and planes of Coastal Command. The sea was best described as 'winter north Atlantic' and all were soon in

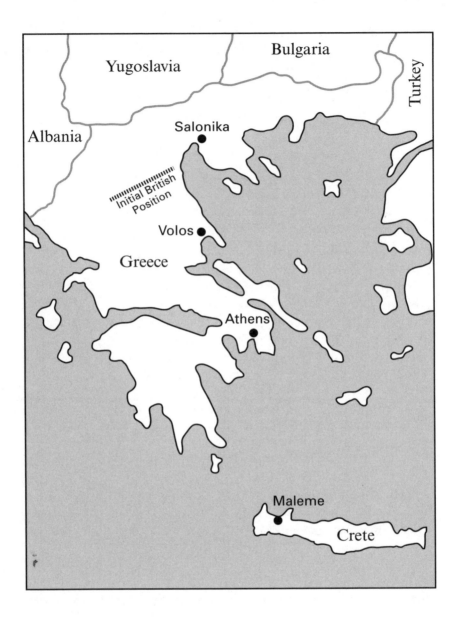

heavy weather; the destroyers appeared to be getting a tremendous dusting in their endeavour to keep station with the larger ships. After several days steaming without event on a southerly course, speculation as to their destination was narrowing down, so that when a town was seen on the port bow, ablaze with lights,

130

Spain became a fairly safe bet. The following morning found them at Gibraltar.

Spirits fell as the rumour of garrison duty gained currency, but rose again when the party was not allowed to land. Thursday, Friday, Saturday and Sunday passed at the anchorage without orders, but on Monday morning at 3.30 a.m. they were turned out of their bunks, paraded on deck and split into two. This mystified officers and men alike, until they were told that they would meet again at the other end. At this stage the officer commanding handed over a duplicate set of orders to his second-in-command and an hour later half the contingent transferred to HM cruiser *Southampton* with the remainder going to the cruiser *Manchester*.

It was 7.00 a.m. when they weighed anchor and headed out on an easterly course into the Mediterranean. On the assumption that they would not pass through the Suez Canal, the geography of the trip was by now narrowed down to one of several possibilities.

During the first day at sea the weather became pleasantly warmer and life seemed a lot brighter than during their time in the Atlantic. Shortly after leaving, the senior captain made a signal to the convoy that as his primary objective was to get the soldiers through without loss, if he fell in with enemy forces, he would therefore take evasive action.

On Wednesday morning at 11.00 a.m. enemy ships were sighted in force and all military and air force details, other than the senior military and Air Force officer on each cruiser, were ordered below decks.

Commenting afterwards upon the captain's tactics, Major West vowed that his idea of evasive action was true to form, i.e. to go full speed ahead in the direction of the enemy! Both forces were closing at high speed until, at 12.40 p.m., the enemy opened fire and both cruisers were straddled by the opening salvoes. Having lived with coast defence gunners, where after bracketing the target the third shell usually gets home, the soldiers felt convinced that they were for it this time. But apparently this is not the drill with Italian gunnery. The cruisers opened with their 6-inch forward guns; the *Southampton* making her mark on a destroyer which was crippled and went down. Early in the action *Southampton*'s forward ammunition hoist was out of action and the sappers were put on manhandling shells up to the gun which gave them a thrill, even if their hands were sore afterwards!

Both sides continued to close in and a fairly heavy general engagement was soon in progress. That grand old ship of such fame, so often sunk by propaganda – *Ark Royal* – was in the convoy and during the battle a returning aircraft reported damage to an enemy battleship and also a cruiser.

By this time all ships, destroyers, cruisers and battleships alike were firing furiously and aircraft from the *Ark Royal* were joining in the general mêlée.

During an action a broadcast is made throughout the ship as to what is happening, chiefly for the benefit of the engine room staff and others below decks. In *Southampton*, this opened with the encouraging remark that if it was not 'guns before butter it was at least shells before lunch'. The enemy was referred to as the Imperial Italian Navy until at 1.15 p.m. when they broke off the action and fled; the commentator then announced 'The ruddy wops have had enough'.

Meanwhile the two cruisers of the Royal Navy put up a terrific chase going flat out in order to force a conclusive action upon an unwilling foe. This left the heavies behind and before long the destroyers were forging ahead of the cruisers in pursuit; the last salvoes were fired from the latter ships at about 1.30 p.m.

Soon after this the humorous broadcaster came on the air again and announced 'a warning to our army friends aboard that Mussolini will most certainly be annoyed when he hears of the Italian "victory" so be prepared for air attack!' This turned out to be a very fair appreciation for at 5.00 p.m. forty enemy bombers came into sight. They made a bee line for *Ark Royal* which was by now on the starboard quarter of *Southampton*. The bombs fell round her and clouds of spray, rising again and again, shut her from view. Fighters literally weaved their way in and out of the bombers and engaged them with much success. After several had been shot down, the remainder followed the tactics of their ships and beat it for 'sunny Italy' and safety. A few hours' peace ensued in which the convoy again took station and continued its passage eastwards. Writing in his diary one of the officers jotted down a few lines from Omar Khayyam, 'the dogs do bark, but the caravan moves on'. This just about expresses the position in a few words and might have been written for the occasion.

However, the Italians certainly tried even if their efforts were not crowned with success, for that same night just after dark, a torpedo attack was staged by enemy submarines. Fortunately they had no more success than their fleet or air force. All the same, it was generally agreed that they had had a fairly full day, with enough adventures for the most sanguine of the party.

The following morning found the *Southampton* and *Manchester* in company with the Mediterranean fleet steaming in battle formation, held by our party to be the most inspiring spectacle of their experience either before or since. There they were, as far as the eye could reach, a challenge to the Italian assertion of '*mare nostrum*'. Passing Malta in the morning, one of the troopships left the convoy and headed for that celebrated bastion of sea power, the remainder steaming on eastwards. On Friday the two cruisers carrying our party, after exchanging signals, left the fleet and steamed southwards towards Alexandria, arriving there in the early morning of the following day. After a brief spell the sapper party exchanged ships and, having transferred all personnel and stores, took passage for Piraeus.

Soon after landing in Greece, one of the largest staff cars imaginable drove up and disgorged a 'brass hat', complete with field boots and spurs, red gorgets and several rows of decorations. He was from the British Military Mission and he announced that the party would become part of the British force that had landed. This resulted in West being taken off to see the senior British Commander. Here the sapper mission was explained and for the meantime, they found themselves quartered in the Hotel Acropolis. The next day another staff officer arrived and said that their first job would be to install electric bells in the place. After having travelled some thousands of miles and having had a conducted passage through a naval battle, this seemed a complete anti-climax and hardly their primary role. As West remarked afterwards,

133

*I shall never forget the look on the CSM's face when I told him to detail the men for our first job ashore – his only remark was 'Coo'. He might well have said more and expressed less.*

Complications ensued over explosives; for some reason or other they had not arrived in the stores ship, which necessitated an officer being flown back to Alexandria via Crete. In due course, however, the demolition stores turned up.

The next job which fell to them was the preparation of camp sites for the incoming British troops. Meanwhile several of the officers attired in plain clothes of approved local cut and style, worked their way up country and reconnoitred the objectives.

Shortly after this a demolition school was opened for Greek officers, to enable them to delay the enemy by spreading the doctrine and practice of a scorched earth policy. They were apt pupils and became firm friends. Our party conceived during the bitter struggle which followed, the highest admiration for the Greek soldiers and civilians alike, particularly the *Evzones*; the highlanders of that ancient race. When the time came near, West, the OC party, found himself in command of a steam yacht, complete with crew, his officers and men, explosives and stores and under orders to deny the enemy the use of certain installations and port facilities. Before leaving, Major West was also given instructions by the senior naval officer, an admiral, to carry out certain tasks in connection with the port and its shipping and to use his initiative as the situation might demand. Finally, with signal details and a wireless transmitter aboard, they steamed out of Piraeus harbour and up the coast towards Salonika.

The background to this deployment of our detachment was complicated. The Italians had attacked the Greeks from Albania but had suffered a humiliating reverse. Hitler came to the assistance of his Italian ally by invading Yugoslavia to enable him to reach Greece. Britain had a treaty with Greece and was in the process of sending three divisions there to support the Greek forces should the Germans invade. They were taking up a position hinged on Mount Olympus, halfway across the country but south of the wide northern coastal strip, which was considered indefensible with the resources available. However this coastal strip contained the large port of Salonika and it was to there that most of our party was dispatched well away from the main British Force.

While at sea they were picked up by a solitary Stuka which made three attempts to knock a hole in the vessel. Fortunately they escaped and, apart from a single Messerschmitt that sprayed them with machine-gun fire, they arrived at Salonika without casualties.

Once at the port, West contacted the British Consul and also a naval officer and put them in the picture. He conveyed his instructions, both naval and military, and outlined the future course of contemplated action. Several British ships were loading in the docks and their captains were instructed to expedite the work and to sail as soon as possible.

At this juncture there was trouble with the crew of the yacht due, no doubt, to the hazards of their previous passage, so they were paraded ashore and addressed through the medium of an interpreter. They were a mixed bag, the captain being a white Russian, the mate a Greek, with a Maltese bosun and a Russian engineer. The remainder of the hands were drawn from various Levantine countries. All our officers were dressed as Greek civilians and most of the sappers were in battledress, so it was a picturesque parade, if not up to the normal standard. The only common factor among the assembly was hatred of the Hun; developing this theme in an address, West made some impression as eventually all said they wished to die rather than forsake the cause. As there seemed a very fair chance of their wish being granted in the near future, it did not take much persuasion to get the crew aboard again.

During the next period much had to be done in order to get accurate information on all the objectives, entailing many tiresome journeys by launch, steamer, in cars, mule cart and on foot. About the middle of March they had all their plans complete and stores spread around the various objectives, but apart from their primary mission, they had many incidental tasks in the common cause. An amusing discovery was that the title 'naval officer' was an emergency measure only; in point of fact, he was a local resident working on our side, the only thing nautical about him being his disguise!

One of the many urgent jobs undertaken was the purchase of £15,000 of tools and stores likely to be useful to the Army. This included such items as steam rollers, timber, etc. and our side found themselves in competition with German agents doing much the same thing. This was a sticky job, usually conducted with libations of local wine, an armed escort and a rear party to keep an eye on the opposition.

At the end of March the swastika was still flying outside the German consulate in Salonika, although the situation was tense and street fights were fairly common. At this period all our officers put on uniform and the men were given shore leave, which steadied the situation a bit in the town. Up till then their only recreation had been swimming and sailing in the bay.

About this time Greek base HQ was about five miles north of Salonika and our Allies were holding the enemy pressure. Meanwhile other Allied forces were digging in around Mount Olympus, about sixty miles to the rear. Contact was established with the British liaison officer who was with the forward Greek HQ and twice daily an intelligence report was collected by an officer. The liaison officer then sent an urgent message by dispatch rider stating that there was nothing between the enemy and Salonika, as they were evacuating present positions. A request was also made that our party should take the dispatch rider with them, as there was little prospect of his being able to rejoin his unit.

Eventually the enemy put in a sustained attack on the forward positions, forcing the pace with overwhelming air power, which resulted in the OC of the sappers receiving an urgent summons to the new Greek HQ. When he arrived he was informed that the Germans had broken through in several places and the situation was obscure and deteriorating rapidly. He was instructed to be prepared to destroy anything of value to the enemy, using his own initiative and to get the Consul and his party away.

By now all our men were on their objectives and the stage was set for the final scene. The OC arranged for the Consul and his staff to be evacuated by the same steam yacht in which they had

136

come up from Piraeus while the sappers commandeered two caiques for their own use. Air raids over the city became more frequent and fierce in intensity, mainly directed against the civilian residential quarters of the town, but in the absence of enemy land forces, the sappers held their hand in the hope that the tide of war would turn. Where the help could come from was not apparent, but it was just a chance. Then signs of increasing fifth column activity, and the evil weapon of rumour became manifest, which could only portend one thing. At this stage they made wireless contact with Athens and received the information that the whole position was obscure. The signal ended with 'Act on your own initiative in face of enemy – Good Luck'.

The remaining few hours were devoted to evacuating as many refugees as possible from the port and, as usual on these occasions many pathetic scenes were witnessed. Incidentally, Yugoslav, Japanese, Polish and Czech Consuls and their staffs were put off in one small steamer which was generally adjudged to be a fair replica of the Tower of Babel, or as one of the sappers observed, 'like the ruddy League of Nations itself'.

Final arrangements for demolition were complete, except in the case of one oil installation where the manager had pro-Axis sympathies. Up to this point nothing could be done, but now the course was clear and, after ten minutes brisk engagement by our chaps, the place was in their hands, all the defenders having either been killed or driven off.

As the Germans entered the town, they managed to blow up or fire all their objectives. The petrol refineries were left ablaze from end to end; many industrial plants were wrecked, including a brewery, engineering works and machine shops in the area of the docks. The gas works were wrecked and left burning; similarly a large flourmill was fired.

In the docks, cranes, locomotives and rail wagons were destroyed and dropped over the quay into the harbour. Stacks of timber and all warehouses were set alight and water mains outside the area cut. In those last few hectic hours a large power station suffered the same fate. Craft of all description were either sent to sea or sunk in the harbour. The spectacle of that scene of desolation and destruction, with its raging fires and pall of heavy black smoke drifting away across the landscape was impressive.

By a marvellous stroke of good luck, on the seaward journey from Salonika, they met another of our sections that had been at Volos about 100 miles south of Salonika. There the Germans had heavily bombarded the place and had, themselves, destroyed the oil storage plant of the Shell Company. This enabled the British party to cooperate with a Greek Naval Commander in the destruction of a fort; guns were put out of action and magazines blown up before leaving. When the various sections of the party met at Athens they all had the same report to deliver to higher authority.

But Athens did not turn out to be a rest camp. With the enemy sweeping through Greece, small parties went forward to destroy an aerodrome under construction at Arexos and to blow up bomb dumps and petrol stores. This was a heart-breaking task indeed as thousands of pounds worth of valuable machinery had been sent out from home to assist our Allies in their war effort. But there was no alternative. It had to be done rather than make a present of the equipment to the Germans. There can be no half-hearted application of the scorched earth policy when it becomes a necessity and is dictated by the military situation.

The Greeks put up a magnificent fight and as is now generally recognized, were more than a match for the Italians in spite of the latter's boastings and propaganda but, when the largest military power on the continent delivered that treacherous blow on their flank, there could only be one end. Although our Allies fought with courage and tenacity, it was only a matter of time, and 'time' was certainly not on their side in this case.

In common with others in the Expeditionary Force, the party sustained casualties and in fighting a rearguard action to the beaches some were captured, but a large proportion got away and was evacuated to Crete.

Chapter Sixteen

# MIDDLE EAST

The party that left us and went to Greece had a fairly lengthy follow-up to their adventures in that historic land. They escaped to Crete where, after a few days respite they were in the war once again. Several thousand airborne German troops came down from the skies and after a very hard fought battle the Germans got a foothold when they seized Maleme air field. They were then heavily reinforced by air and the capture of the island was inevitable. Some were taken prisoner and sent to Germany. Among these was Second Lieutenant Dennis Alabaster, a young regular officer who had joined us at Gravesend, he managed to escape from a POW train and joined the Chetniks in Yugoslavia. Sadly we heard through our Mission that he had been killed in the fighting there. Others of the party sleep their last in the soil of Crete, but it is the remainder who escaped that concern us here.

The majority of our party got away under cover of darkness and steered a course for safety. They had water but very little food; nonetheless friendly craft helped them during the course of the passage. Providence was kind in the matter of a fair wind, and the blue waters of the Eastern Mediterranean treated them well.

Except for the glare that harassed their eyes and the attentions of enemy aircraft during the day, it was not a bad passage. Sometimes these planes would fly low and suspiciously circle the craft only to make off apparently satisfied; on occasions they would liven up the proceedings with a burst of machine-gun fire, but without serious results. The men would lower themselves over

139

the side for a bathe to cool off. There was much talk about the meals they were going to have when they got ashore. The nights were cold and with the exception of the watch the human cargo huddled together for warmth. They eventually landed safely.

The survivors were initially stationed in Palestine, that land of contrasts where ancient civilization meets rocky barrenness and a fringe of cultivation here and there joins the sweltering coastal plain.

For a time a detachment left for Syria and were mixed up in the fighting against French Vichy Forces. One incident subsequently commented upon in official dispatches was when the officer in charge, together with a corporal, were flown behind the enemy lines and landed near a steel girder bridge vital to the opposing forces' withdrawal. Under cover of darkness the following night, they stealthily approached their objective and, overcoming the guard on the abutment, laid their charges. With the first streak of light, 'when dawn's left hand is in the sky', they blew up a span, withdrew to the agreed rendezvous and were flown back behind our lines. This journey back was interesting as they passed over a full scale engagement between the opposing forces, and saw below what resembled a cloth model of a battlefield. 'Just one more job'.

But life was not to continue on these lines, and before long they were back in the building and lading side of their craft. Seemingly endless miles of roads were the order of the day, sometimes with all modern mechanical aids, but not infrequently just humping and shovelling, much as the ancients had done for centuries; real back aching work. However it was not without its compensations, for the food was good, fruit and vegetables plentiful and tobacco easily obtainable even if of a peculiar quality and flavour. Cigarettes were said to be made of 'camel droppings and palm fibre' although in due course it was said that the fibre had become scarce.

Some months went by and prospects became dull. It looked as if they might end their days on chores, but their luck remained good and the welcome order arrived, transferring the party to Egypt, this time by orthodox method of transport and without adventure. Thereafter the party was absorbed into the MEF and with that force shared the vicissitudes of the desert in many months of striving against the Afrika Korps and nature in the raw; hundreds of miles backwards and forwards over the grim theatre of war, where the sun blisters by day and the night chills to an unbelievable extent; where the all pervading sand finds its way into everything. There were the flies, a myriad of pestilential creatures that made life almost unbearable at times. This was their lot in common with the gallant Eighth Army. The place names that have become almost commonplace in the world news such as Alamein, Agheila, Tobruk and Benghazi were, to these men, oft recurring milestones in a campaign of sweat and blood.

There was the continual movement of eternal packing up, striking camp and off again due to the ebb and flow of battle. They were faced with a harsh climate, a depressing country and a relentless enemy. The continual probing for soft spots and manoeuvring for flank attacks which went on unceasingly, has earned the desert credit for being the 'tactician's paradise'. This may sound well in journalism, but ask the troops and they will tell you the choice of noun is unfortunate.

Sometimes these sappers were under the command of larger units; at other times they were out in small detachments on a variety of tasks that can only be listed by reference to the RE pocket book (with amendments!).

Then there were the mines, tens of thousands of them, either to be put down or taken up, to say nothing of that invention of the devil, booby traps, which had to be cleared or disarmed according to the direction of movement. Small parties had to go forward under cover of darkness and crawling through the enemy minefields, locate, lift and pass back those engines of death to the rear. They were then disarmed and, in the case of our own minefields, made safe for subsequent re-issue. The mine belts were frequently a quarter of a mile deep, protected with all kinds of tripwires and anti-lifting devices. Also they were sometimes irregularly laid which made detection difficult. They were invariably covered by both shell and machine-gun fire which would come into action at the slightest sound. The task was one for quiet stealth, iron nerves and a firm belief in your ability to

141

beat the Hun at his own game. The result of these mine gapping parties left lanes cleared and marked for the assault through the minefield.

These lonely sapper parties carried on this task night after night, intent upon their work, for it is not the kind of occupation which encourages thoughts to wander. You only have to make one mistake, for death peers over your shoulder all the time. Every conceivable method of minelaying to prevent detection and lifting was practised by both sides and quickly mastered by the opposing forces.

The whole question of supplies to this nomadic force will probably come to be regarded as a wonder of organization but in one aspect alone, that of water supply, the task imposed upon the sappers was gargantuan. For many weary months they were employed on this struggle with nature; well-boring, pumping plants, filtration and chlorination installations. On occasions no water could be found and it had to be brought forward in four gallon tins by RASC transport. Sometimes behind our positions, at times well forward and not infrequently out in the blue; at times a rough and ready job, but at other times a highly developed engineering task of some magnitude. Two things never changed; the demand for more water and the necessity to follow the tide of mobile desert warfare. As one of the sappers remarked after many months on these tasks, 'Just imagine if the people at home kept pulling up the ruddy water mains and re-laying them'.

For one period the sappers were employed upon the construction of dummies to deceive the eye of ever watchful enemy reconnaissance aircraft, for in the desert with its high sun, heavy shadows and colourless background, camouflage means something more than just throwing a camouflage net over a vehicle. There are dummy positions, dummy vehicles and guns, in fact dummy everything at times to outwit a wily foe, all of which means a lot of preparation, hard work and organization at improvised workshops which follow the actual fighting in this arid theatre.

The highlights of this peculiar existence were those occasions when mail arrived from home, work was laid aside for a brief moment, thoughts went back to town and country in England. The all absorbing personal details of wife and children gripped the imagination and transported the reader back for a few brief moments to his normal life. The desert fades for an instant, and the surrounding mirage seems to be of streets or country lanes, even the flies are forgotten in this all too brief period of suspended animation. The silence gives place to a buzz of chatter when confidences are exchanged, a few remain silent, very silent, the unfortunate ones who did not receive a letter, when suddenly someone comes on the scene and urges forward the job in hand. Letters are put away for subsequent re-reading and the working party is back in the war on the same old tasks. The flies irritate once again and the heat blisters.

Sometimes during the unhappy days when withdrawal was imposed upon the army, they would be back at their old role of demolition. Benghazi and even Tripoli were the objectives always uppermost in their minds even in the dark days; on these occasions they felt instinctively a reluctance to destroy such facilities that existed as the whole army was convinced that ultimately they would succeed in returning westwards.

The tide of war at last turned. Attack and advance was the order of the day and the sappers of the Eighth Army took part in the spectacular and decisive victories which led up to the great advance from the Egyptian frontier through Cyrenaica, Tripoli and on to Tunisia.

Some of our men were present when Winston Churchill made his historic appearance at Tripoli. They saw the kilted pipers swing through the town to the skirl of 'The Road to the Isles' – (this was a favourite tune of our own band in those far-off pre-war days) and in this strange setting of pageantry, thoughts not unnaturally turned to home. Others were on the roofs in the town, looking down between the palm trees on the Prime Minister of England reviewing the armoured might of the Eighth Army from a staff car and then, from the saluting base. The gunners, sappers and infantry, all swung past, spick and span with no evidence, save perhaps their tan, of the 1,000 mile trek and weeks of fighting in that memorable advance from El Alamein. The presence of our Prime Minister at this psychological moment of success acted like a tonic upon officers and men alike; never was a visit more appropriately timed. The only laugh was that twenty-four hours later, after Mr Churchill had left, the Hun put in some fierce bombing attacks. Presumably their intelligence was a day out for once!

Chapter Seventeen

# AIRBORNE

It is well known that in 1940 Winston Churchill, shortly after becoming Prime Minister, ordered that we should form a corps of not less than 5,000 parachute troops. For a start No. 2 Army Commando was sent off to Chesterfield and to the small airfield at Ringway which became the Parachute School, to form a nucleus of the corps. Army Commandos were formed from volunteers from all Arms and so there were a number of sappers in No. 2 Commando. It was going to take months to build up to the Prime Minister's target, as they were starting from scratch and, in due course, the call went out for volunteers.

In the autumn of 1941 an officer in our unit HQ volunteered with several of the soldiers and went off to join Airborne Forces. He was Captain Stephen Dorman. Before the war he had been a preparatory school master and joined the army at the outbreak of war. He had fought with an Independent Company as they were called, the forerunners of the Army Commandos, in Norway. (Dorman had joined us in Gravesend in 1940.) He was tall, very tough and deeply religious and impressed everyone immediately by his sincerity and integrity. At this time the decision was taken to form a special Airborne Sapper unit in its own right. Dorman commanded the so called Air Troop Royal Engineers and when this was expanded he became the Commander of the 1st Parachute Squadron RE. Sadly this courageous man, whom his soldiers so liked and admired, was lost on a one man patrol at night in North Africa and was never heard of again.

The Holding Company consisted of a surplus collection of officers and men over and above the ordinary Field Companies, to supply a pool of men to provide parties for 'jobs'. They trained in the arts and crafts of sapping and mining, with a special bias towards offensive demolitions; it was a peculiar mixture of unarmed combat, coupled with skill at arms. The company contained some of the Lord Wakefield rifle team of 1939, and a number of well-known county shots, who had gone to Bisley Common to earn a dividend in those elusive prize lists, in the far off days of peace. Physically they were a tough lot, lads who could find their way about by day or night and if needs be, could live off the country.

The formation had come upon another dull patch and for some weeks had been employed upon the construction of tank traps on a particularly exposed portion of the Irish coast. It was a wind swept place with driving rain and lacked all amenities. The men worked long hours and slept in tents, when they were not blown down. Temporary cookhouses and Soyer stoves shared the same fate. For all it was a case of hard work coupled with life in the raw. In their ranks were young men who had experienced something of a Cook's Tour along the northern seaboard of Holland, Belgium and France; small wonder then, when, with the changing fortunes of war, the character of operations changed from withdrawal to attack, orders came through for conversion to a Parachute Squadron, RE. This was the end of the 'Hot and Cold' (Holding Company) but the beginning of a new chapter in their history.

In the spring, the CRE of the embryo 1st Airborne Division visited the company, inspected all ranks, looked into their record and offered a welcome to all who wished to volunteer for the winged badge of a parachutist. Some of the unit had already volunteered for Airborne Forces.

The CRE was Lieutenant Colonel Henniker, later Brigadier Sir Mark Henniker. In his autobiography *An Image of War* he states:

*Early in 1942 2 Parachute Brigade was formed under Brigadier Down, who had formally been the CO of 1 Parachute Battalion. This Brigade needed a sapper Squadron and a new method of raising it was devised. A good Territorial Field Company in Northern Ireland was selected and 'converted' into 2 Parachute Squadron. Any officer or man who did not like the prospect could opt out and go to another unit. I therefore went over to Northern Ireland and had the Company assembled to tell them about it.*

*I took with me my driver, Driver Low, who had come from 253 Field Company. I thought, rightly as it turned out, that he would be a good recruiter. The men were assembled in a dining hall and I told them of the proposal. Following Gideon's example I dwelt more on the hardships than the joys. I told them of the discipline required of a parachutist, and the spit and polish, the drill, the physical training, the route marches and all the things most calculated to discourage the faint hearted. The men listened in stony silence until I had finished. I then told them they could have a few days to discuss the prospects amongst themselves, but as a matter of interest I should like to see how they felt at the moment by a show of hands. Almost everyone in the room put his hand up signifying his willingness to become a parachutist. It was a wonderful spirit. In the event many men had to be rejected on medical grounds, but there remained a first class nucleus with an esprit de corps and a Territorial Army tradition second to none. The Sergeant Major was a particular character. A middle-aged man, a pre-war Territorial and far too old for the job, he asked to be allowed to stay as Company Sergeant Major when the unit was converted. With many misgivings I gave the necessary permission and the CSM came over with the others to 1st Airborne Division in Bulford. He remained with the unit until the end of the war, a most outstanding success and a tribute to his own stout heart. He was a GPO Engineer by trade. Their Officer Commanding was a tall, thin Major from the Territorial Army named Paul Baker. He overcame the teething troubles of conversion to the new role but had the misfortune to suffer a serious motor accident in North Africa before going into action.*

The Sergeant Major referred to by Colonel Henniker was 'Daddy' Weeks. He was known as 'Daddy' on account of his age and he wore on his chest the Great War ribbons. He was not in fact a GPO employee as stated, but was the foreman of the Packing Plant at the Blue Circle Cement Works from which nearly all the other ranks were recruited.

As might be imagined, it caused some surprise when, as a prelude to their new training, all ranks were put on 'toughening and hardening' for several weeks. It was an orgy of PT, running, long marches and games; a most enjoyable interlude before the serious business began. This phase accomplished, the company said goodbye to Ireland and re-crossed to their native land.

Then came the days of ground training in which the embryo parachutists had to learn how to make a good exit from aircraft, how to control the descent once the parachute opened and lastly to make a good landing-drill second nature. In the training school were many types of equipment especially designed to familiarize the learner with all the physical and psychological reactions to leaving an aeroplane in flight, the journey down and, finally, contact with mother earth once again. The training layout is known as the 'circus'; rather an apt description as our party soon discovered. Split up into small 'sticks', each group came under an RAF instructor to practice rolling, swinging, falling and jumping from the most peculiar gadgets designed to render the trainees parachute conscious – the consensus of opinion appeared to be that it was like the funfair at Margate, only more so (much more so)!

When the learners began to get accustomed to their harness and surroundings and learnt how to fall without injuring themselves, they were introduced to Heath Robinson contrivances which looked sufficiently fearsome to inspire a fair degree of doubt but were, in fact, graduated to the physical and mental development of the students. All the time strenuous PT and lectures formed a background to produce high morale, fitness and efficiency.

Then came controlled descents in harness over short drops. The learners jumped through a hole in the floor, where the speed of going down was checked by mechanical means and the acceleration of gravity is not precisely as the text books describes.

After some weeks of ground training came the first real jump from a captive balloon. All agreed that the emotions on the upward journey were mainly centred on averting eyes from the hole in the floor. A kindly thought on the part of the designer of this outfit relieves the beginner from having to open his parachute, so he jumps out through the hole and gravity does the rest. A few seconds drop, then a tug at the shoulders and, lo and behold, he floats gently to earth!

At last came the real thing. The 'stick' marched to the bomber, was inspected by the Commander and entered the waiting plane. The machine took off and the chaps began to wonder what they had let themselves in for! At times they sang, then came the warning on the intercom, 'Ready for Action' followed, a few seconds later, by the green indicator light. One after another, in their right order and without fuss, they quickly disappeared through the hole in the Whitley bomber. At first little sensation was experienced, due to being in the slipstream of the plane, then a bit of buffeting, followed by the familiar tug at the shoulders, and lastly the descent. Once on the ground the 'stick' hastily detached their chutes and went straight for the containers for arms, ammunition and explosive equipment for the job in hand. The care and attention given to obtaining the greatest value for the least weight in rations and all airborne equipment would surprise most soldiers, who either walk on their feet or are transported by ground vehicles. It is a magnificent training where physical fitness and careful organization go hand in hand to ensure every chance of success in action.

Perhaps the most exciting experience in the training is the first night operation; even the approach to the familiar airfield takes on an eerie appearance with a half moon playing hide and seek between low cumulous clouds. The emplaning, now familiar enough by day, seems distorted with the heavy shadows, and the rest of the 'stick' look strangely awkward fellows in their kit. The customary command is followed by the revving up of engines into a roar. The take-off restores thought to the usual subjects and procedure. The flight is, of course, much the same, with the great difference that outside all is dark; the fitful moon only seems to accentuate the blackness. Then the exit into stygian gloom, anxious searching earthwards but nothing to see; down, down, it seems longer than usual, until quite suddenly they are on their feet again. Within a few seconds, numbers of the stick join each other and start their ground tasks just as though they had arrived there by any other means. The tang of the cold night air and the dew upon the ground is nature's stimulus to quick thought and action on these occasions.

When the required number of drops had been performed the men were awarded their cherished wings and some leave. At last these lads from Kent joined the ever increasing throng of dapper young men who wear maroon berets jauntily on the side of their heads and mingle with the crowds wherever service men are to be found. Their life upon the ground is much the same as any other soldier, except for the special emphasis on the rapid exploitation of an opportunity. This entails great fitness, thorough training and an eye for the main chance.

The squadron had lectures and demonstrations of previous operations from the first raid in Italy in the attempt to destroy an aqueduct, to the Bruneval raid and later work in Tunis. Much was to be learnt and, as in all dangerous undertakings, a fine understanding between all ranks and pride of craft was developed in this new branch of the Army. It would be affectation to deny that they had solid grounds for their pride, in between time, they still sing about Mr Stevens, Windy Notchy Knight and piccanin skoff. Maybe some airborne sapper with a lyrical bent will write a verse more appropriate to his new method of arriving on the job.

There for the moment we leave the Kentish Airborne Sappers in the full assurance that, as in Tunisia, so elsewhere they will render a good account of themselves in the destruction of the King's enemies.

Chapter Eighteen

# *UBIQUE*

Over three years have now passed since the original Territorial Army sapper unit, whose deeds and service are recorded in the foregoing pages, embussed at their local drill hall to man their war stations in the Thames Estuary. They have added a page to the records of their Corps in carrying on in almost every theatre of war, in a manner born of the traditions of the British soldier. Time must of necessity bring changes but the spirit carries on and the unit, although now greatly diluted by reinforcements and expansion, still retains individuality even in this vast concourse of fighting men. They are carrying on their trade of lading, building and holding weapons as ordained in all theatres. A hard core of the young men who, in the early days, feared they would miss the excitement of war still remain.

One contingent formed part of the force that landed in Morocco, that vast armada that showed the world the combined sea and air power of the Allied nations. The surprise landing and fighting with Vichy elements is too recent to permit recapitulation. The airborne paratroops included representatives of the old unit too: soon no doubt, those from the east may, by chance, meet these new arrivals in the west in some mess or NAAFI and the tongues will wag to the accompaniment of such local cheer as is available.

Looking back, one is instinctively amused at our impatience during those early months when we sat in those dreary old forts, and watched the tides ebb and flow over those acres of slimy mud flats. How desperate we became to get on with it. Our lot didn't seem good enough. We went through the various cycles of training, boredom, indignation and almost despair; so great was our self pity at the hardness of our portion and the humdrum nature of our existence. But our chance came.

While it might be argued that the foundations were laid on the barrack square, these adventures ashore and afloat have developed a fine understanding between officers and men. After all, you cannot be shipwrecked with a man, or both soaked in petrol and make your way through a burning oil plant without getting to know each other pretty well! This is something more than *esprit de corps*; it is confidence in each other born of experience to see the job through. This happy outcome has been a great encouragement to us all.

It is a far cry from Spitzbergen to the burning sands of Libya and from Amsterdam to Salonika. France too seems a long way off in these days, but the fact remains that war has taken those impatient young men, who a few years ago complained of the dullness of existence, and spread them far and wide.

Some are prisoners, a few are guerrilla fighters, the remainder carry on in one or other theatre of war, whilst a proportion sleep in deep waters or in foreign soil; a number wear the ribbon of some decoration.

Surely there is a moral to the story, particularly for all young soldiers who feel that life, for the time being, is in any way dull:

*ALWAYS KEEP ON YOUR TOES; YOU NEVER KNOW WHAT IS JUST ROUND THE CORNER!*

# EPILOGUE

It is sixty-three years since the events recounted here took place. Reading it now I am struck by the feeling of the almost complete isolation that these parties faced, especially in the operations in the Low Countries. They were small groups commanded by junior officers operating completely on their own. They were landed on foreign shores where invariably the countries were in chaos and in a near state of collapse from the German blitzkrieg. They had no covering force as such, no communications to higher authority, little food if any, no provision for the evacuation of casualties, in fact no re-supply of any kind and most important of all psychologically, no return ticket. In these operations, except later on the Seine, where they were placed across the lines of communication of the British Army, no mention or provision was made for their evacuation. In those days there was no magical gadget like a helicopter to pluck them out to safety at the last moment, although the Navy, true to form, took great risks to try and get them out.

The other aspect of these operations which strikes me, as a sapper myself, was the crudeness of the equipment which was all that was available to them at that time. The serious limitations were that gun cotton slabs were always difficult to secure in a hurry, blankets soaked in kerosene to fire heavy bunker oil were the only means of ignition in some cases and first aid stretchers were all that they had to carry their demolition stores. Despite all these difficulties the will to succeed triumphed.

These operations happened at the beginning of the war. Only a year or two later plastic explosives were developed which could be wrapped around objects to be attacked, incendiary devices

153

containing magnesium were freely available, likewise delay fuses which could be set to operate from a minute or two up to a few days. Lightweight canvas and aluminium trolleys, developed for airborne forces with drag ropes attached allowed small parties of men to move considerable loads manually.

As a matter of interest the only special provisions made for them in respect of weapons were that each section, roughly one officer to ten men, was equipped with two Boys .5-inch anti-tank rifles and about half the men had .38 revolvers as well as their rifles. Both these weapons were in critically short supply early in the war and their allocation was not ungenerous.

For those of a military background it will come as a surprise to hear that this small unit received their orders <u>direct</u> from the Military Operations Branch of the War Office. This must have been unique, as orders normally always come down the chain of command. This was probably due to the extreme secrecy of these operations and the speed with which they had to be set up.

The Kent Fortress was expanded in 1940, as is explained in the narrative, into Kent Corps Troops Engineers and on the disbandment of HQ 3 Corps in Northern Ireland in 1943 they became 15 GHQ Troops Engineers specializing in bridging. They bridged all the major waterways through France, the Low Countries and Germany in 1944–45. Second Parachute Squadron, the old Holding Company, served in North Africa and Italy and took part in the airborne landings in the south of France in 1944 and later in Greece. On demobilization nearly all the original hands returned to their roots in the cement industry. Several of the junior officers were made works managers on their return to the Blue Circle Company and, in due course, Peter Keeble became a director of the company. My father left the company and went out to Northern Rhodesia to build up and run a cement works there. He returned to England in the early 1950s and set up as a consulting engineer. He died shortly afterwards in 1959.

Grain Fort, which features in Chapter One and was the HQ of the Thames and Medway defences, was bulldozed in 1953 to make way for the building of the oil refinery on the Isle of Grain.

Attitudes in those days were less melodramatic and this was typified by remarks made in a letter from Commander Goodenough congratulating Peter Keeble on his DSO. He ended the letter thus '. . . after working in the Plans Division in the Admiralty the Amsterdam party was just like a paid holiday'! Commander Goodenough had received an immediate DSO.

Don Terry, the junior officer who went to Amsterdam, drove to the site of the refinery from Germany in 1945. There he met a group of middle aged women who well remembered the firing of the oil stocks. They admonished him for not giving them any warning which would have enabled them to get their washing in; it was ruined as a result!

After the war the Dutch authorities salvaged the bullion lost in the River Maas near Rotterdam. A British film was made about both its loss and recovery although the film had little to do with reality.

In Chapter Nine – 'Robinson Crusoe', one of the castaways, was Corporal E. Baker. He was commissioned later in the war. In 1982 he returned to Kervenny and their island refuge. The older inhabitants well remembered the incident and their local school mistress drove Baker about fifty miles to see the priest in his new parish. It was an emotional meeting, a bottle of champagne was opened and they sat down to a mini banquet. When Baker returned to Kervenny the next day, he went out to the island which was now uninhabited and the cottage derelict. The kindness of the priest in 1940 lives on in all their memories.

P.H. Brazier

# ROLL OF HONOUR

The following men from the Kent Fortress Royal Engineers laid down their lives in the service of their country during the XD Operations in the Low Countries and France in 1940.

| | |
|---|---|
| Corporal H.E. Ayers | Lost on the *Lancastria* |
| Sapper H.W. Blackman | Lost on the *Lancastria* |
| Acting Lance Corporal E.G. Brown | Lost on the *Lancastria* |
| Sapper G.A.V. Haines | Died in the Forest of Blain |
| Sapper S.J. Owen | Lost on the *Lancastria* |
| Acting Lance Corporal E.E. Plummer | Lost on the *Lancastria* |
| Sapper S.J. Ruck | Lost on the *Lancastria* |
| Lance Corporal Shute | Lost on the *Lancastria* |
| Sapper A.H. Wells | Killed in Action, Boulogne |

Appendix II

# HONOURS AND AWARDS

*(For the operations in the Low Countries and France)*

Plate 27 is a newspaper cutting from the *Gravesend and Dartford Reporter* listing the honours and awards. As the local paper, it was natural that they should show great pride in the exploits of their local Territorial Unit. Not mentioned on this list was the MC awarded to Second Lieutenant B.J Ashwell for his exploits at St Malo as he was not a local man.

What is of interest is that my father recommended Keeble, Goodwin and Buxton for MCs and these were approved by the Director of Military Operations. This fact is in the National Archives (formerly the Public Record Office). Churchill, who had only just become Prime Minister, had, up to May 1940, been First Lord of the Admiralty and during that time had become very concerned about the oil stocks in the Low Countries falling into enemy hands. It is understood that when he was informed of these successful operations he was greatly relieved. He sent for a report and having read it, put a pen through Keeble, Goodwin and Buxton's citations and deleted MC and wrote DSO across them. It must be appreciated that these junior officers not only showed great leadership but in all cases they had the heavy responsibility of carrying out their instructions despite opposition in many cases from very reluctant and difficult senior Allied commanders.

Appendix III

# PROPOSALS FOR THE DESTRUCTION OF BULK OIL STORAGE INSTALLATIONS

It is understood that as early as 1939 concern over the fate of the oil supplies in the Low Countries was expressed in Whitehall. First thoughts were to hand over their destruction to the RAF should it become necessary. Tests were carried out with practice bombs on areas laid out to simulate these targets. The results were very disappointing. At that stage in the war bomb sights were extremely inaccurate and the bombs could not be dropped with anything like the necessary precision. Therefore there was no alternative but to employ ground parties to undertake this task.

Oil storage tanks are typically 120 feet across and 50 feet high. As a safety precaution they are invariably surrounded by an earth wall or bund so if by any mischance a tank should become ruptured, the fuel would be contained within the bund and not allowed to spread all over the surrounding area. Considerable thought was given as to the best method of destroying these large tanks with the limited resources that would be available to small parties of men on foot. It was fairly obvious to start with that it would be impossible to set fire to the storage tanks when full as there would be no oxygen for combustion. Therefore it was appreciated that, without enormous demolition charges, igniting the fuel would have to be done in two stages. Firstly, the tanks would have to be partially drained and when sufficient oil had been released, this could then be fired. To achieve this, the following possibilities were considered:

a.  All tanks have small drain cocks at the bottom to drain off any water from condensation and these could be opened but this would be a very slow way to let the fuel out.

b.  Manhole covers might be removed but this would be slow and access could be a problem.

c.  Should it prove difficult to get access to the storage tanks for any reason, several half inch holes could be shot into the tanks with a Boys anti-tank rifle and after sufficient fuel had run out, it could be ignited by firing tracer into the liquid.

d.  The most favoured solution appeared to be to blow off the exit valves leading out of the tanks with a slab of gun cotton. These weighed one pound and would have to be secured in place with adhesive tape.

So much for the proposed method of getting the fuel out of the tanks into the bunds. All these tank farms held stocks of petroleum products ranging from light aviation fuel through the various grades down to heavy bunker oil. The tanks might be either situated singly or in small groups behind a common bund. They now had to consider the best method of igniting the fuel and being able to withdraw safely. The first and fairly obvious method to be used for petrol tanks and groups of tanks where at least one was petrol would be the firing of a Very Light cartridge up and over the liquid to ignite it. Where there was a mix of grades of fuel in tanks behind a single bund, it was considered that the petrol, being lighter, would flow over the heavier fuels. Tanks of heavy bunker oil on their own would be a separate problem. The best method appeared to be to soak blankets in kerosene, of which there was a plentiful supply in every refinery, and lay several end to end over the bund and into the heavy oil; both a fuse and wick in effect.

# INDEX

Lord Wakefield rifle team, 146
Low, Driver, 147

*Maidstone*, HMS, 122
Mailleraye, 48
*Malcolm*, HMS, 32
Maleme air field, 139
*Manchester*, HMS, 133
McKye, Commander, RN, 82, 83
Meyler, Lieutenant Roy, 48, 122
Milton Barracks, 12
Mitchell, Sapper, 68
Mount Olympus, 134, 136

Nantes, 58, 60, 62
Narvik, Battle of, 24
Neufchatel, 54
Ny Alesund, 118, 119

Ouistreham, 77, 78
Owen, Sapper S.J., 156
Owens, Second Lieutenant, 80, 88

Parachute School, Ringway, 145
Petit Couronne, 48
Plummer, Acting Lance Corporal E.E., 156
Port Jerome, 48
Pyramiden, 118, 119

Ramsay, Admiral, 23
River Brest, 54
River Maas, 25, 28, 155
River Scheldt, 16, 33
River Seine, 40, 43, 66, 80
River Thames, 98
Rotterdam, 16, 25, 28, 32, 155
Rouen, 40, 43, 44, 47, 48, 53, 54, 55, 57
Ruck, Sapper S.J., 156
*Rye*, SS, 79

*Sabre*, HMS, 78
Salonika, 135, 136, 138, 152
Savenay, 58, 60, 61, 62
Shell Company, 138
Shelton, Sapper, 78